Sex and Rhythm

A guide for experiencing metaphysical sexuality through rhythm.

Marie Laveau

By Steve Paige

Steve Paige
SEX AND RHYTHM

ISBN: 9798727285046

Steve Paige
SEX AND RHYTHM

Steve Paige
SEX AND RHYTHM

Contents

Steve Paige
SEX AND RHYTHM

Introduction to Rhythmical Sexuality

This is a book about sex with no illustrations and no gimmicky how-to information. It will be the oddest book about sex you have ever read. That's a good thing. What I propose is that there is more to sex than we normally assume. There is a spiritual component that can be accessed by you with some willfulness.

Gender differences, which we will refer to often, assumes that there are two different instinctual needs between men and women that most people are vaguely aware of. Some would claim that there is a gradation of differences between men and women. To those I would say that this is probably not the book for you. The off-putting title is a validation of a sexual minority among the super straight heterosexual community. This book assumes there are metaphysical adjuncts associated with sex between a man and a woman. Others may write about similar relationships gendered differently. That is not my interest here. I purely write from my own experiences as a straight male musician.

Instinctual drives are built into our unique hormonal responses to situations we encounter with each other. It has not been until recently that science has been able to see how this process works.

Mostly, this scientific investigation goes on without any relation the to what people claim on social media, who are not scientists. These scientific findings are so important to you and me, that they can completely change our thinking about the opposite sex.

By reading this book, your take on the 'battle of the sexes' won't require as much negative energy from you as it does now. Hopefully after you read this book you will be a little more accepting about other people's sexual values and your own changing needs and desires. I have written this book for the average reader. Many of the experiences and processes described in this book are related to sexuality and enhance the sexual experience without being specifically sexual or involving how to methods mechanically about sexual organs. This book is more about peripheral experiences involved in the development of a vigorous sexual response with metaphysical goals.

I have simplified as much as I can the present science of how each gender is influenced by their respective neurochemical response systems. These differences have evolved over millions of years. They are as absolute as the visible physical differences between men and women which some claim does not exist. This book is for those who believe there is a difference. I hold great compassion for those outside this understanding without any thought of demeaning them or censoring them. Internal neurochemical differences between men and women do exist. With the advancement of imaging medicine, genetics, and neurochemistry, we are now able to look at our basic instinctual differences in much the same way as we enjoy looking at our physical differences. The joy of it is that we are just as interesting and attractive to each other on the inside as we are on the outside. To understand how men and women interact together you will need to understand in basic terms, the basis of 'mood' or 'desire'. We react differently. We make the analogy that neurochemicals are like background noise for the control of your moods, motivations, and desires.

Each sex has own internal hormonal and neurochemical programming. Science has determined that the gender differences in neurochemical makeup between men and women affect behavior and social interaction of the two sexes. Much of the most recent changes in the sexual politic between men and women have been induced by changes in communication. Musical and iconographic communication carry hidden instinct and gender changes in our neurochemical response. Music affects the instinctual needs of each gender. Music in this book is presented as a form of continual foreplay. We back up this claim with behavioral science and ethnographies. Technological advancements have made musically expressed sexuality a primary driver of the polemic shift into a world ruled by feminine instinctual needs and behaviors. To comprehend the sex as music interrelationship I ask for a little forbearance with respect to what you take for granted about your concept of time.

Defining Time.

What if many of the adepts of Tantra before you were born assumed a different concept of time? What if that concept allowed them quicker advancement in their journey to heart and hormonal coherence with their partners? Is there something in the spontaneous nature of rhythm and music that involves another relationship to time? What is improvisation? What secrets are held by the spontaneity of music?

Are we more than just a thing? There is scientific proof that all the atoms in each of your 36 trillion cells in your body are replaced completely every 15 years. Who are we claiming to be me? Can it be inferred that we are not something material if we exchange atoms constantly? If we replicate every cell in our body every 15 years what is there of the original self? How do we have memories among this atomic recycling? The answer may surprise you. All life is made up of dynamically changing energy fields represented in the moment by more stable but interchangeable atoms and molecules.

And as for memory, the only thing that could be 'remembering' is your repeating energetic fields. Yoga describes these fields as 'Chitta' or 'field' of consciousness. Scientists have used Carbon 14 dating to be able to measure how fast cells change from their original atoms. We must assume our energy field is stabilizing our 'self' and recreating 36 Trillion cells constantly with great accuracy. The fact of cellular recreation leads us to assume we are dynamic recurring energetic fields, not 'matter' or 'self' or something solid moving through time. In fact, time does not exist. Time is a social construct. But I will get to that later.

The energy field of a thought is so slow relative to our cellular intercommunication it is impossible for us to perceive the instant complexity of our energetic universe within. Nestled within the vast energetic relationships that make a thought is a whole universe of reverberation starting with subatomic particles. Our consciousness grows out of vast energetic interactions going at a scale and speed that is almost incomprehensible. This inner frontier is important in understanding our place in the universe and the rules that govern it.

At a near zero fraction of a second the Universe is frozen like in a snapshot. Even the fastest subatomic movement is stopped. The probability of energetic recurrence or repetition becomes zero. Out of that zero point, which we have no scope or knowledge of directly, the universe instantaneously arises creating an ever-changing energetic interrelationship.

Consciousness is the synthesis of infinite energetic repetitions in and around us. Energetic fields nest within each other. Nesting is visually like one Russian doll within another. The atom is an energy field nested within a molecule. The molecule is nested within a cell. The cell is nested within the body. The earth within the solar system within the galaxy. Basically, one energy system can be nested within another. Energetic fields entrain and amplify each other while others cancel each other out. It is the basis

13

of holography. Harmonic cellular light fields transfer information in energetic cellular systems. Mostly we think of sound when we think of harmonics. But the full energetic spectrum of the universe can exhibit harmonics. The universe is more like a piece of musical vibration.

At an infinitely fast pace, energetic rules of creation are manifested at speeds that are unfathomable to us. Creation itself approaches in it's a vast array of associations an event horizon of non-recurrence. So, when we speak of consciousness we are speaking of a level of complexity and energetic repetition that is merely a pattern evolving out of what is unknown to us. Our sensory awareness is precluded by a vast array of cellular energetic events. They are built on a vast array of molecular and atomic events.

Atoms themselves are mostly energetic fields where mass behaves as both a wave and a particle in creating an electron shell. The shell is not solid. The exterior of the atom is built up of a repulsive energetic field that nests with like fields in a matrix. The atom itself is mostly empty and devoid of mass. The nucleus of an atom is infinitesimally small compared to the energy field of the electron shells. Measurement of atomic events runs up against abject uncertainty about the behavior of electrons because they will not follow a standard set of physical principles. Mass and energy become interchangeable.

Consciousness on a cellular and molecular level is for the most part filtered from our awareness. Cells are several degrees closer to our energetic horizon or zero point of energetic motion. Our 36 trillion cells are operating at a repetitive energetic bandwidth that is much faster than we can consciously perceive. Cells 'talk' in complex fields of energetic interaction at speeds well above 200,000 informational transactions per second per cell! These transactions give off energy that creates fields of energetic patterns that are multicell informational matrices of light and electromagnetic energy.

You can see remaining traces of these patterned fields in a simple physical experiment for yourself. Your mind operates at about 60 hertz or sixty frames a second. Cells individually operate as a field matrix at around 200,000 hertz where one chemical transaction is one energetic broadcast of information to surrounding cells. Recent science even proposes that DNA is a mirror or antenna in these communications. Multiply that by 36 trillion cells in an individual body you can see that consciousness is immersed in infinite energetic complexity, transferring a matrix of information at the speed of light made mostly of infinitesimal energetic fields (atoms).

Here is a test. In a darkened room cup your hands over your eyes without pressing on them to create total darkness. Now, look off as you would into the distance. You do not see total darkness. What you see is moving or stationary patterns, gray on black, mauve on black, green on black patterns. What you are looking at is the subtle energy fields of communicating rod and cone cells within your own eyes and your brain's interpretation of them. All the cells in your body create these informational fields. They are conscious and communicating with their neighbors and expressing an energetic group think as

15

informational fields of electromagnetism and light. Because of their size, complexity, and speed of communication, to us, they are beyond our sensory horizon. They are piecing together and adjusting the energetic puzzle of consciousness. They absorb energy and turn it into a changing dynamic field of harmonic and homeostatic energetic association. A small part of these energetic associations is our sense of consciousness. Like a piece of complicated music, our total being is playing an 'instant' song of infinitely complex energetic cohesion in the ever-present now.

What if I claimed you could tap into the rhythm section of this universal orchestration? Tap into it in the now. First, I would have to convince you that there is only the present. The depth psychology of Tarthang Tulku the Tibetan scholar in the book <u>Time, Space, and Knowledge</u> outlines a methodology to perceive only the present as time. An alternative to this philosophical approach is to learn rhythm as a meditation. Rhythm will show you how to unwind your sense of time into the present.

You have only to look at the anthropology of time to understand that it is *a shared social contract* in the present. The artifacts of our obsession with time are colossal but only exist in the instant as a sum of many stable energetic recursions. By 8 Billion people agreeing on what time is in the present we can imagine or dream the idea of the past *in the present.* Time only exists in our collective consciousness as an idea.

Time is intrinsic to our language so escaping the concept of time is difficult for you. But with rhythm you can do it. The fact is that many cultures do not have past, present, and future descriptive verbs. The

Praha tribe that lives in the Amazon rainforest base their language on whistling and humming. They have no concept of time. Everything exists in the present for them. The Hopi also have a language that lacks verb tenses, and their language avoids all linear constructions in time. The Hopi appear to have no sense of linear time. Their religious beliefs include a cyclic view of time, like ancient Hindu and Buddhist belief in the "wheel of time".

We are constantly having to manipulate time to account for our observations of the Universe. Einstein's theory of relativity stretches and compresses time to accommodate his observations and mathematical formulas. Wheeler-DeWitt equation was devised by John Wheeler and Bruce DeWitt back in the 1970s. They attempted to unify relativity and quantum mechanics. Their final solution resulted in time essentially disappearing completely from their equations. Unequivocally proving time was unnecessary as a concept to describe complex interactions of energetic particles, space, and mass. Black holes stop time mathematically. This social agreement is ever-changing and, in some cases, doing away with time altogether. So how do we understand existence without time?

The three dimensions of space are merely juxtapositions and nesting's of energetic repetition in the NOW. An atom in you is juxtaposed to a molecule, is juxtaposed to a cell, is juxtaposed to an organ, is juxtaposed to a body, is juxtaposed to the solar system, is juxtaposed to the Milky Way Galaxy. Size, proximity, and energetic repetition can explain our world without the concept of time.

17

We can assume consciousness is a stabilized energetic field of nested and heterodyning energy. Perception of consciousness is instantaneous. It is based on recurrence of energy patterns we cannot perceive. Awareness is global, thoughts and memories are discrete energy fields nested in global awareness. Global awareness makes no distinction between self and non-self. There is no within or without because all energy is interrelated.

We learn thought and memory from the total field of human interaction. All human interaction is a nested co-dependent global energy field also. It is a field that has learned to manipulate 'matter' bound in a more stable energetic relationship. It is why if you are put in solitary confinement you eventually cease to have organized thoughts or memories. We all are one with the Universe because it is unwinding with us in the ever-present moment.

The term used to describe this human co-dependent field phenomenon has been developed through scientific investigation. Theoretically it is called 'Morphic Resonance'. The theory has been developed by Rupert Sheldrake PHD to explain instantaneous telepathy and global learning at a distance among other phenomena. The theory claims not all thoughts are in your head. They are intrinsically linked to the total of human consciousness by 'morphic resonance'. Using the vernacular, we developed above, they are nested, clustered, and heterodyning energetic fields of instantaneous common 'thought'. Thought is claimed to have a life of its own, outside our 36 trillion cell core colony of what we refer to as 'self'.

18

Collective social consciousness about time has allowed us to instantaneously manipulate the longer and shorter recursion rates of all matter and energy, big and small. Collectively we are like the conductor in an orchestra. By embedding thought and action into recursion and position of inert matter the collective consciousness of humanity has stabilized collective thought as a habit of interaction. The concept of time is part of that habit. But time does not exist. Our ego and sensory horizon gives us limited access to the instantaneous recursive mega-fields of life force and the Tao of the universe. Everything in the eternal instant becomes connected to the whole. Existence is more like a song than an object. It is a song you can play for each other in harmony. That is the song of Rhythmical sexuality.

Sexual Attraction.

We must understand just a little bit of science of perception to understand the changes in cultural expression of gender due to music. We are taught nerve transmission by little electrical impulses. But there is another kind of nerve response, neuromodulation by the bodies free floating nerve enhancers circulated in the blood and fluid outside our cells. They are composed of a stew of hormones, neurotransmitters, and pheromones. In classical models of nerve function nerve information is transmitted from cell to cell through adjoining boundary layers called synapses. Electrical impulses travel along this chain of nerve cells to the brain where the information is processed. The whole cycle from initial simulation to awareness takes just a fraction of a second. This is the normal nerve transmission that you read about or are generally aware of.

Less well known but clinically validated is the nerve process called Neuromodulation. Between any two nerve cells is a small space called the synaptic boundary. Imagine that the synaptic boundary is a hallway with two doors on either side. You want to pass a message from one room to the other. In the hallway are 150 or so messengers all with their own agenda. When you pass a message from one room to the other, in this case from one nerve cell to the other, each messenger garbles the message a little bit to fit its own agenda. Some messengers pretend to be other messengers.

Some messengers won't cooperate if there are rivals in the hallway. It gets complicated. Anyway, on a cellular level your sensory perceptions are being altered by the hormonal state of the space between any two nerve cells. The messengers are called in science hormones, neurotransmitters, and neuropeptides. It is now understood that hundreds of synaptic modulators are always circulating the hallway affecting your perception. You are not even aware of it.

The thing about these neuromodulators is that they are persistent. Where a standard nerve impulse takes a bit of a second, neuromodulators can change every nerve impulse to fit its needs for hours. These metabolic changes are commonly referred to as "states of consciousness" or moods. The states of arousal, inhibition, fear, hunger, thirst, sexual desire, sleepiness, comfort, etc. are triggered by changes in the proportioning of different neuromodulators in our body fluids that are addressed to specific locations in the body. That way your body and mind can communicate with each other in a visceral way, so you do not forget to sleep, eat, or be interested in a little hanky-panky.

Certain areas of the body are targeted by these neuromodulating substances. In science these target areas are referred to as neural nodes, neural receptor sights, or neural networks. In this way nature can efficiently prepare a state of consciousness by merely releasing a particular group of neuropeptides into the body fluids. Not only do you miss out on the whole process intellectually, but the process also actually controls what you think. The release can occur from many different locations in the body but most notably from the sex glands and hypothalamus commonly referred to as the ancient brain.

Some neuropeptides (messengers in the hallway) are time dependent like LH, FSH, estrogen or progesterone responsible for the female cycle. And some neuropeptides are stimulus dependent like, endorphins, endo-opiates, oxytocin, epinephrine, and adrenaline. So actual sensations and perception of sensation is altered continuously at the synaptic level by neuropeptides that are constantly altering your "mood". This in turn controls your behavioral choices in a very subtitle way. You don't often associate these changes in perception with what you consider rational choice. Yet they subvert your choices by altering your 'mood' and perceptions on a cellular level. My analogy is that these neurochemical messengers in the hallway are like software programs operating in the background of your mental activity and moods.

Homeostasis- Your comfort zone.

Reproduction is a good example of a regular cyclic process driven by circulating hormones and neuropeptides. FSH and LH, two female hormones act on the ovaries and cause the release of the female estrogen and progesterone. The increased hormone levels also induce changes in cell structure and chemistry that lead to an increased capacity to engage in sexual behavior. The feminine cycle is mirrored in the male cycles increase in testosterone in a chemical coordination between the two sexes.

Balancing this time-oriented dance of hormones is the ultimate built-in neurochemical release system meant to coordinate our moods and desires. Women are instinctually driven to situations that reinforce and regulate the hormonal balance of their sexuality programming. The internal drive to balance the FSH LH birthing dynamic we call the drive for feminine homeostasis.

Homeostasis means a relatively stable state of equilibrium between the different but interdependent changing elements of an organism. Homeostasis equates for our understanding, to balanced biorhythms, normal sexual desire, urges to nurture and be nurtured, successful childbearing, and urges to enjoy maternal care. Feminine homeostasis is intricately woven into the cycle of life and cultural development. It also mirrors the cosmology of the lunar cycle. Many feminine instincts and behavioral choices have evolved to protect feminine homeostasis and reinforce, and in some cases re-boot the chemical software program.

These feminine instinctual drives to reinforce homeostasis are the feminine side of a behavioral polemic between men and women. Men often misread or ignore homeostatic signaling between females. Women have a complex economy of behaviors that protect and enhance homeostasis that men do not normally see or have the desire to be a part of. Homeostasis is generally enhanced by a stimulus-oriented neurotransmitter called oxytocin. Sexually practicing partners exhibit oxytocin enhancement for each sex. But this neurochemical relationship is highly dependent on early life interactions between the mother and sibling via breastfeeding. Adults that did not have close contact with the mother at this early age have to work harder as to safe harbor their relationships via oxytocin release. Women signal their partners constantly about the conditions of their homeostasis.

Early Enhancements

The biochemical bond between a mother and infant pre-wires consciousness for feminine homeostatic cultural validation and perception. The first contact a child has with the world is with his or her mother. Basic hormonal and neurotransmission pathways of the infant are set for life. Hormonal receptor sites are created, and synapses are grown controlling the emotional and physiological interactions of the infant's life experience.

Through direct physical contact with the mother and breast-feeding infants arrange their experience around sensations like, warmth, touch, eye contact, comfort, security, sustenance, body rhythm, and cyclical awareness. The infant's body senses these experiences and responds by adapting his or her neurological growth.

Neural growth is directed to integrate with neuro-motor activity associated with the positive sensual bond between mother and infant. When an infant experiences endorphin, and endo-opiate enhancing sensations then the growth of these receptor sites is biologically encouraged. The positive experiences are imprinted on all levels of consciousness; sleep, awake; conscious, unconscious; active, passive. They are also imprinted on body-time strengthening and integrating body-time with the mother. The baby drops into the biorhythms of the mother.

This is the imprinting of cyclical, integrative, consciousness. The more entrained the mother and infant become, the more the baby's biochemistry integrates the process of bonding and consistency of his or her physical needs being met. The baby's neurological system develops in parallel with its neural input, lowering the threshold for positive pleasurable experiences. These thresholds follow the infant on into adulthood creating a loving individual that understands and desires to re-live the experiences of comfort, physical affection, mutual sensory synchronization, and Conversely, if an infant is deprived of positive maternity, receives poor physical contact and is also given food only when expressing primal scarcity, then the infant is biologically preprogrammed for survival and stressor states of consciousness. They are also unable to relax and integrate pleasurable experiences in later life.

These substrates of consciousness dictate a framework for all life experiences of the individual. When our culture embraces and supports infant maternal bonding and nurture, we complete a subtle circle of connectedness. The rewards of this connection are so pervasive that they completely alter perception and communication. These basic positive physiological experiences support positive family and community from generation to generation through their direct application to consciousness.

Deep maternal bonds change the balance of power within the family structure. These bonds ask us to accept and redefine how openly women can express themselves as mothers, not sex objects. The weight of knowledge we have about infancy and motherhood crushes many popular notions about child raising. Foremost is what we know about breast-feeding.

Breast-feeding and breast milk are best for infants. Still many women experience a lack of support when it comes to breast-feeding. Many women are determined and breast-feed no matter how much society or their own families do not support them. Then again, many women can't handle the rejection and humiliation that our ignorant culture puts upon them. Health care workers, constraints in the workplace, misinformation from the infant food industry, society, and yes, even family members oppress and exploit women's ability to breast-feed.

It is rare that a woman would not produce enough milk for her infant. If a woman can breast-feed right after delivery, no supplemental bottles are given, and she does not smoke, it is very unlikely that she would not produce enough milk. This misconception is thought to be true because breast-feed infants require more frequent feedings than bottle fed infants. Newborn infants basically only do a few things well. One of these things is suckling, so if given a bottle after breast-feeding the infant would probably drink it. People do not ask if calves get enough milk from their mama cows, and they certainly would not recommend supplementing with a bottle of human breast milk.

Human breasts manufacture milk that is perfect for humans, unlike cow's milk that is perfect for cows. Cow's milk contains a different type of protein than human breast milk. This is good for calves, but human infants can have difficulty digesting it. A similar problem arises with formula. Many infants can be allergic to formula because it is synthetically produced. No babies are allergic to their mother's milk. Human milk contains at least 100 ingredients not found in formula. Human milk contains just the right amount of fatty acids, lactose, water, and amino acids for human digestion, brain development, and growth.

Breast-fed babies are healthier and have fewer infections than formula-fed babies. A mother's antibodies to disease are transferred to her infant through breast milk. About 80 percent of the cells in breast milk are macrophages, cells that kill bacteria, fungi, and viruses.

Breast-fed babies are protected in varying degrees, from several illnesses, including pneumonia, botulism, bronchitis, staphylococcal infections, influenza, ear infections, and German measles. Mothers also produce antibodies to diseases they meet. They pass these antibodies on to their infants to protect them. A breast-fed baby's digestive tract contains large amounts of Lactobacillus bifidus, beneficial bacteria that prevent the growth of harmful organisms. Breast fed infants is not exposed to bacteria because breast milk is sterile.

Breast-fed babies also have fewer problems associated with their mouths. There are fewer dental carries associated with breast-feeding because breast milk does not pool in the mouth like liquid from a bottle. A baby must suck to get milk from the breast, unlike a bottle that will keep running no matter what.

Breast-fed babies also have fewer inner ear infections because of the position they are held in while being nursed. Milk does not easily run into the Eustachian tube next to the tonsils that controls inner ear pressure, because the baby is held up to the breast so that the milk runs into the esophagus. The tendency to lay bottle fed infants down flat with a bottle propped against with a blanket so that their head is turned to the side, allows milk to flow right into the Eustachian tube. There is however a study linking cancer of the esophagus in children linked to women with implants who breast-fed.

When women's reasons for choosing bottle-feeding include fears that breast-feeding will alter the shape of their breasts, then women are accepting being treated as sex objects. How did breasts become defined as sex objects for male pleasure rather than as the source of food and comfort for children? What about the benefits mentally and physically that breast-feeding has for women?

Nursing requires extra calories that were gained as weight during the pregnancy to be used up faster. Nursing requires a lot more calories to be burned than would be burned mixing formula. Breast-feeding also stimulates the uterus to contract, this allows for the uterus to return to its normal size faster and eliminates the need for painful manipulation of the uterus after birth.

There are also studies that link breast-feeding with a decreased risk of breast cancer among pre-menopausal women. Frequent breast-feeding also suppresses ovulation; making it less likely for breast-feeding mothers to menstruate, ovulate, or get pregnant.

Breast-feeding creates a bond between mother and infant. This bonding is biochemical. The suckling infant cause hormones related to the impulse to bond and nurture to be released into the mother's circulatory system. Breast-feeding also allows for the mother and infant to experience sensory input of warmth, comfort,

28

and security. Both the release of oxytocin and the sensory response after birth have been cited as reasons for positive effects. The hormone oxytocin is a hormone released by the thyroid gland. Its release has a broad range of effects on the mother. Among these are: strengthening of the uterus, milk let-down, increase of milk producing hormones, and the physiological impulse of bonding to their infant. Increased contact with the mother also promotes regular breathing patters and heart rates for infants. This decreases the chance of crib death. It also decreases the practice of putting an infant in a room by itself at night, because the infant will also require feedings at night.

Breast-feeding a child beyond one year is a major taboo in our culture, because we adults obviously equate breast-feeding with sex. Yet, the worldwide average age at weaning is about 2.8 years. In societies where children can nurse if they want, they usually self-wean, with no arguments or emotional trauma, between 3 and 4 years of age. In terms of the benefits of extended breast-feeding, there have been a few studies comparing breast-fed and bottle-fed babies in terms of the frequency of various diseases, and I.Q. achievement. In every case, the breast-fed babies had lower risk of disease and higher I.Q.'s than the bottle-fed babies. There are also tremendous emotional benefits for the child being able to have that emotionally secure bond with their mother. Breast feeding builds pathways for enhanced Neurochemical transmission and neural node alteration. It builds the synaptic and limbic basis for communicating with pleasure. The Oxytocin enhancements from nursing creates limbic memory of pleasure and bonding that becomes a future sexual bonding and mating enhancement and strategy.

Oxytocin

The oxytocin response from breast feeding carries over into later life sexuality. Oxytocin is one of the messengers in the hallway. In men its effects are reduced by the hormone testosterone. Women have a broader range of behaviors that enhance oxytocin release that then in turn helps strengthen homeostasis. Positive social interaction triggers oxytocin release in women. This explains why women react so positively to live music and musical idols. I t explains why women s e e k out common company of their own gender.

Strangely, monogamous romance induces oxytocin release, but it fails to be produced in women having the same amount of sex with many different partners. This explains why they are normally interested in serial monogamy rather than random sex with strangers. Regular exercise increases oxytocin production. Oxytocin lowers blood pressure, lowers blood level of stress related hormones, reduces response to stress and promotes the healing rates of wounds and improves sexual response (Uvnas-Moberg, Psychoneuroendocrinology. 1998 Nov;23(8):819-35).

Oxytocin release has powerful influence on mother infant bonding, induces milk production, and causes contractions of the uterus during breastfeeding which returns the original muscle tone of the uterus after birthing.

So, you can see how even this one neuromodulator manages to influence a whole set of behaviors and physical responses in women. Oxytocin alters nerve perception and mood on a cellular level. Oxytocin mediates, enhances, and signals the body to strengthen the complex feminine cycle. Oxytocin drives behaviors that reinforce homeostasis.

Endorphins

Drug like self-made opiates called endorphins also enhance homeostasis. The human body produces at least 20 different endorphins with possible benefits and uses that researchers are investigating. Beta- endorphin appears to be the endorphin that seems to have the strongest effect on the brain and body during exercise; it is one kind of peptide hormone that is formed mainly by Tyrosine, an amino acid. The molecular structure is like morphine but with different chemical properties.

Endorphins are believed to produce four key effects on the body/mind: they enhance the immune system, they relieve pain, they reduce stress, and postpone the aging process. Scientists also have found that beta-endorphins can activate human NK (Natural Killer) cells and boost the immune system against diseases and kill cancer cells.

Short-intensity workouts like sprinting or weightlifting do not increase endorphins. Prolonged, continuous exercise like running, long-distance swimming, aerobics, cycling or cross-country skiing, or dancing appears to contribute to an increased production and release of endorphins. This results in a sense of euphoria that has been popularly labeled the "runner's or dancers high."

The blissful feeling you often experience after making love is due to the body's production of endorphins: in fact, endorphin production can increase 200% from the beginning to the end of sexual activity. Recent studies, beginning with those of Candace Pert, Ph.D. of Johns Hopkins University, have documented the connection between orgasm and endorphins, although ongoing physical contact, and not just sex alone, also helps produce endorphins, along with the hormone oxytocin.

To auto regulate homeostasis, behavioral choices are made by women that enhance endorphin release. Social situations that encourage endorphin release are running, going to the gym, walking, and dancing. Long dance experiences, dance aerobically for over an hour, can create a natural high. Raving, club dancing and historical long dancing or dancing marathons encourage endorphin triggered euphoria, without drugs or alcohol. Endorphin enhancing experiences are sought out by women unconsciously to reinforce homeostasis. Quite often these female goals are not strictly sexual. Modern advertising takes advantage of the drive for homeostasis which is why many products are juxtaposed to soothing music and personal sensuality.

Music and Testosterone

Testosterone, the primary male sex hormone, is needed also in smaller quantities by females. Testosterone is used and approved as a topical agent to improve female sexual desire. In a recent study, it was discovered that listening to music increases testosterone levels in women making them more sexually aggressive and sexually motivated. Testosterone is also assimilated by smell and skin to skin contact. This pheromone exchange is another generator of homeostasis driving feminine behaviors. Pheromones are odors that are unconsciously exchanged between men and women. Both living with a man or living with other women will trigger dynamically balanced hormonal response in women.

Pheromones from men, testosterone being among them, change hormone levels and mood in women. This affective response occurs in heterosexual relationships. Proximity to male odors caused changes in the feminine cycle hormone LH causing increased estrogen levels, and increased oxytocin levels. Being around male odors auto regulates the feminine hormonal cycle. (Preti, Wysocki, Barnhart, Sonheimer, and Leyden) Women who live in proximity and unconsciously share body odors with other women will synchronize their fertility cycle and induce group hormonal homeostasis.

Researchers have found that odorless compounds from women in the late follicular phase

33

of their menstrual cycles accelerated the preovulatory surge of luteinizing hormone of recipient women and shortened their menstrual cycles. Compounds from the same donors which were collected later in the menstrual cycle (at ovulation) had the opposite effect: they delayed the luteinizing-hormone surge of the recipients and lengthened their menstrual cycles. Nature. (Stern K, McClintock MK. 1998 Mar 12;392(6672):177-9.)

In music listening experiments, the testosterone level in men goes down and the testosterone level in women goes up (Fukui and Yamashita, 2003.). This makes men more cooperative and women more sexually aggressive in a musical environment. Women need small amounts of testosterone. Testosterone is causally related to the feminine sexual response. It is used topically as a treatment for female impotence and depression.

Music effects cardiovascular tone by accessing the ancient areas of the brain bypassing language. Music lowers blood pressure and reduces stress hormones. More importantly music directly affects all important endocrine neurotransmitter nodal points. (Sound therapy induced relaxation: Down Regulating Stress Processes and Pathologies Salamon et al. 2003)

Music is like an elixir for feminine homeostasis acting like a broadband signal that triggers oxytocin, endorphin, testosterone, and Nitrous Oxide onto the synaptic bridge between nerves and into the brain itself. No conscious thinking about music is necessary for this to happen. The stimulus of music causes these effects automatically because the process evolved through natural selection over a long period of time and is basically cellular.

Many of us are familiar with Nitrous Oxide use at the dentist's office or recreationally in dance venues. We also create it internally. Internally induced NO creation in the bloodstream materializes on a cellular level as a direct reaction to music. William James wrote about NO; "As with every other person of whom I have heard, the keynote of the experience is the tremendously exciting sense of an intense metaphysical illumination and unity." The music/ NO connection could possibly be related to early man's shamanistic experiences of spiritual illumination and tribal unity. The effect of NO dissolves the sense of isolation between individuals or between each gender. These could have been our first experiences with music. Music came first, complex language second, writing third.

Scientists at the prestigious Neuroscience Institute in New York demonstrated that music has numerous profound effects via Nitrous Oxide, opiates (endorphins) and the hormonal system (oxytocin, ATCH, melatonin, and testosterone enhancements). Furthermore, NO was shown to be a necessary molecule in the development of the auditory system, which is required to enable music to act as a relaxant. Taken together the article claim's that the complex nitric oxide signaling system is the primary and fundamental method by which music acts as a relaxation device. (Salamon et. Al.)

It's easy to see music reinforces homeostasis by acting as a hormonal regulator. It encourages male cooperation, female sensual excitement, euphoria, and a sense of unity. Tightly knit cooperation of a small group of hunter gatherers and sexual availability would have been favored by evolution. Also mutual embedded cognition of musical movement and dance encourages heightened awareness of nonverbal sexual clues between men and women.

This allows men to access complex rhythmical 'invitations' into the feminine dynamic balancing act that are primarily unconscious and kinesthetic. But more important than that, music invites cohesion on every level, music is a form of broadband sexuality easily related to by women because it reinforces feminine homeostasis just like continuous sex does. Both behaviors evolved co-operatively. Sex is foreplay for feminine homeostasis. Sexual completion is not the behavioral agenda for women, homeostasis is. Sex and music are a means to satisfying a greater behavioral need driven by biology.

Men often interpret feminine sensual interactions in a musical setting as lesbianism or bisexuality when basically they are watching a less understood behavioral reaction related to homeostasis. Sensual dancing is a gentile form of sensual relationship that is different from the male drive to procreate.

For women, gentile touch and cooperative complex rhythmical signaling in dance movement further enhances oxytocin release and pheromone exchanges. That interaction is an end with the primary goal being shared feminine homeostasis. Look around you at female hand clapping games, jump rope, a girl's innate memory of rhymes, music during homework, dancing, and crushes on musical male celebrities. Everywhere, Women seek out music and rhythm to reinforce their sense of safety, sense of community, and homeostatic hormonal balance.

Men bridge into these states of feminine complex sensual economics through music. Let us for the sake of understanding here call the male musical bridge builders 'Musical Shaman'. Musical Shaman can crossover the behavioral barrier of basic gender differences in cognition and body language between men and women.

There are two almost disconnected brain hemispheres. In men the neural path between the two sides of the brain is 30% smaller than the neural path in females. Men use the spatial temporal right side of their brain more than women. Women use both hemispheres of their brains, in a sense, multitasking the linguistic and spatial temporal dominance of each hemisphere. When men learn to play music, not just listen to music, they start multitasking their brain function like women.

Rhythm has been shown to be processed in the right side of the brain. Tone is processed on the left side of the brain. The temporal embedded cognition of rhythm meets the nuance of our primal emotional relationship to tone. Tone carries allot of emotional baggage left over from our evolutionary attention to a baby's cry, and sensual affirmations by our partners. Out of this instinctual attention arose our complex relationship to tonal nuance. Rhythm and tonal harmonics reinforce homeostasis.

Tantric Chakras as Nodal Points.

Certain areas of the body are targeted by neuromodulating substances. These target areas are referred to as nodes and groups of nodes are referred to as neural networks. In this way nature can efficiently prepare a state of consciousness by merely releasing a particular group neuropeptide into the body fluids. The release can occur from many different locations is the body but most notably from the glands and hypothalamus. Some neuropeptides are time dependent like LH, FSH, estrogen or progesterone responsible for the female cycle. And some neuropeptides are stimulus dependent like, endorphins, endo-opiates, oxytocin, epinephrine, and adrenaline. So actual sensations and perception of sensation is altered continuously at the synaptic level by neuropeptides that are constantly altering "mood".

The Chakra System in Tantra is mirrored in neural networks and concentrated nerve Receptor Sites. A strong association can be made between the theory of neural networks and the Tantric theory of various chakras. The well-being of each chakra affects the "state of consciousness". The balance of nodal networks determines "physical states of awareness.

In Tantric philosophy extended sexual meditation is said to open up the Chakras or energy centers of the body. There are six well known chakras. All of them have a psychic component. That is, the person experiencing disruption of the function of a particular chakra has an emotional component

38

and a behavioral relationship to its imperfect function.

The first chakra or root chakra is associated with elimination. Its psychic component has to do with issues of survival. Hence the innate response to defecate during extreme fear situations. Also, issues related to constipation, or diarrhea and obsessive toilet habits may be related to the psychic component of the first chakras energy. Behavioral patterns may imply a need to relive issues related to survival, fear, and fight or flight.

The triggering neuropeptides that network control centers involved

with these issues are Adrenaline and related compounds. It is well known that adrenaline is the neuromodulator involved in the fight or flight response. Adrenaline is a stimulus released neuromodulator. It shuts down many bodily functions so that survival can be dealt with. It interrupts the function of other neuromodulators that are associated with rhythmical cycles of biomodulation like sleep cycles, eating cycles, breathing, and in extreme cases shock and circulatory collapse.

The second chakra is related to sexual function. Many sexual hormones

which is part of the complex of neurotransmitters are time dependent and address certain receptor sites at times of the month, or at times of day. The sexual response itself is time and stimulus oriented and triggers the release of endorphins, endo-opiates, and sex hormones. These sexual neurotransmitters reinforce the cyclic nature of the sexual cycle increasing hormonal regularity and balancing hormonal release.

The sexual hormones themselves are experiential filters that are induced into the limbic system. They too are informational substances that act as filters on our perceptions. Like a chord played on a piano, sex hormones act in symphony with other informational substances that are released by pleasurable sensations and relaxation.

Protective fear based selective attention is filtered out and sensations of pleasurable openness are enhanced by manipulation of nerve cell data on a cellular level. The synaptic response is reformulated to gain our selective attention towards experiencing sex and its related biorhythmic enhancements: better sleep, deeper breathing, lower blood pressure, relaxed muscle tone, emotional bonding and regular digestion.

These biological enhancements to the organism create an altered perceptive reality triggering state dependent memories, associations, and state dependent selective attention. We enter another state of consciousness.

The psychic component of the third chakra is power or life force. The center of this chakra is said to be at the solar plexus. It coincides with the receptor node complex of the digestive system. There is a network of opiate receptors in the digestive tract.

Appetite and weight gain are modulated by endo-opiate peptides. Issues of domination and submission, controlling behavior, and power are often associated with digestive disorders. Anorexia, bulimia, and overeating are disorders associated with behavioral control of digestive functions. Since these functions are dependent on opiate receptors, they will often respond to treatment using hypnosis to trigger opiate enrichment or as tantric believe they can be cleared through opiate enrichment caused by continued sexual stimulation.

The life force is further affected by opiate enrichment of the thymus, spleen and the immune system. Monocytes circulating in the bloodstream are the basic fighters of the immune system. They encircle invaders and destroy them. Monocytes not only have receptors for receiving neuropeptides they also manufacture and emit them. Emotion affecting neurotransmitters appear to control the routing and migration of monocytes in the bloodstream (Ruff). Positive emotions and pleasurable experiences increase the capacity of the immune system.

It has been speculated that neuropeptides provide the psychological basis for the emotions. There is a striking pattern of neuropeptide receptor distribution in the mood regulating areas of the brain. Essentially endorphins, as well as other information substances and their receptors function on many levels from the spinal cord up through the cortical-limbic-hypothalamic system as filters. They modulate all sensory, perceptual, and physiological information. This might be the process by which the conscious mind with its expectations and planning functions can modulate psychosomatic processes down to the spinal cord level.

In tantra this process is metaphorically described as perceiving with the third eye or fifth chakra. The mental imagery or point of meditation in the tantric exercise is encoding all perceptual strata in

41

the nervous system with a new set of neuropeptide filters. This neuromodulation is constantly interacting with classical neurotransmission. The striking similarities between psycho-somatic processes and the metaphors of the chakra system enable us to comprehend the tantric sexual process more meaningfully.

All homeostatic internal regulatory centers from the spine to the hypothalamus are in communication with a vast sexual receptor system. All major behavioral states of attention, motivation, sleep, dreams, memory and all physiological processes like respiration, body rhythms, appetite, autonomic nervous system functions and sensory tuning have associated sexual receptor sites. Estradiol (female sex hormone) and testosterone are networked to these sights when their level is raised in the bloodstream.

Expanded use of sexual energy in the tantric sexual meditation increases these hormonal levels, respectively. When pure thought and physical technique are practiced in tantric partnership selective state awareness is shifted and you experience a new state of consciousness.

Endorphins are enhanced by repetitive breathing and voicing of specific sounds known to tantric as a Mantra. The vibration of the chest cavity from the mantras sounds increases neuromodulation of the pleasure response. The rhythmical breathing increases oxygenation of the blood which sharpens sensual awareness.

The Tantric sexual act itself is a conscious effort between two people to reach an advanced state of selective awareness. Using eye, breath, and movement entrainment, the sexual partnership follows a psychic rhythmical flow that keeps on bathing the receptor system in a constant flood of endorphins, endo-opiates, and sexual hormones. Locking sensation in rhythm without orgasm as a goal allows altered state neuromodulation to build and build.

The result is an advanced state of filtered sensation that triggers a barrage of emotions and awareness's. The physical advantages of sexual euphoria are then encoded into the cyclic functionalism of the body. Including kinesthetic memory and subconscious processes which often triggers lucid dreaming or what feels like magical synchronisms.

The process of the sexual meditation restructures perception in the individual through extended changes in neuromodulation that ripple out through the receptor network of the body. Hence the tantric metaphor of the opening of the chakras is clearly a psychic tool to unleash life enforcing psycho-physical processes at work in continued tantric sexual cooperation.

Early Beginnings

Oxytocin, endorphins, testosterone, and pheromone exchanges are unconsciously sought out by females to bio-regulate. Women have a complex and repeatable sensual dynamic that requires complex sensual strategies to successfully fulfill their emotional and instinctual needs. Are they searching to physically validate hormonal shifts and to reinforce homeostasis? How did men evolve to fit into this complexity?

The male hormonal polemic reflects a man's role as an ancient member of a small tightly knit group of nomadic hunters. For thirty thousand years, men wandered out to hunt and would have to react swiftly and decisively to danger or prey. The men that were a little slow, well we know what natural selection did to them. The men remaining developed a tendency for spatial and temporal thinking required for hunting skills. They also developed a complex behavioral relationship to the neurotransmitter epinephrine the fight or flight neurotransmitter.

Epinephrine or Adrenalin plays a central role in the short-term stress reactions—the physiological response to conditions that threaten the physical integrity of the body. It is secreted by the adrenal medulla. When released into the bloodstream, epinephrine causes many diverse occurrences by binding to multiple receptors in the body. It acts to increase heart rate and strength of contractions, dilate the pupils and constriction of blood flow restricts blood flow in arterioles in the skin and gut. Vessels dilate in the arterioles of the leg muscle and redistributes blood flow away from the skin and inner organs. Men evolved using this hormonal reaction to protect clan, and indirectly, feminine homeostasis. Men have spent 30,000 years socializing this reaction and giving it a contemporary social structure, we all take for granted.

So hormonally men are still hunting and protecting the communal feminine homeostasis of their small tightly knit nomadic tribal unit neurophysiologically. We have outgrown our own neuropeptide reactions. The hormonally controlled traits for establishing territory, aggressive display at the approach of other males, mating, mate protection, sexual competition, and mate bonding that you see in other primates maybe are dysfunctional for man with his present technological skills. Male mechanisms to shelter feminine homeostasis and complete the birthing cycle are related directly a man's ability to moderate epinephrine and testosterone in a socially acceptable way. Music helped him do this.

The same old behaviors are there, but social and technological advancements make them much more complex and dangerous. The original drive to protect feminine homeostasis or 'pride' or 'harem' and to mate and bond in a small community is lost in a history of wars, genocides, technologies and intellectual as well as physical territorialism. All our social systems, religions, and nation states are moderated by social exemplification of male instinctual needs and hormonal precursors.

There is another side of male hormonal energy that is hidden inside 30.000 years of genetic evolution. It does not get much attention. We can imagine what happened when men came back from the hunt, put down their spears and played music, held shamanistic rites, and sought spiritual allays. When male our hunters faced socially inward, they evolved male hormonal strategies that were relational to feminine instinct and moods.

45

Oxytocin changed male behavior too. Oxytocin created from successive sexual encounters, causes bonding, sexual interest, and grooming behaviors in male primates. But testosterone lessens the effects of oxytocin quickly. Sex was a way to renewing oxytocin's behavioral effect on men to encourage them to protect and reinforce hormonally driven feminine birthing strategies. Oxytocin soothed the beast.

Among our nearest evolutionary ancestors, the primates, there is a marked difference between male and female behavior. Male behaviors are noted by their inclination toward expressing the establishment of territory and aggressive display used to establish sexual or physical space. Female behaviors are inclined towards nurturing and cyclic integration.

When male's express territory it is usually over food, hunting areas, or harem (female mating groups). These are not intellectualized behaviors but are genetically encoded in the biology of the of the primate animal. To retain territory the male uses aggression to establish territory: loud noises, pounding, beating, charging, and sometimes-violent acts towards another males, females, or infants.

The major biological motivation behind display and territorial control is the hormone release of adrenaline and related neurotransmitters. These hormones momentarily override and interrupt the other functions of the body. Display reactions and aggression during adrenaline release is a widely recognized response.

Male primate drives for display and territory constantly modify themselves in humans in a large

46

variety of social associations. Humans due to their vast social intelligence have adapted territorial and display behaviors to a wide range of social interactions, just like the socialization of nurturing instincts in females. These two gender specific behaviors create considerably different cultural manifestations when they prevail in religions, myths, worldviews, and social interactions. Women play a small part in the outcome of such aggressions and are usually considered as property to be exploited, owned or violated as an extension of territory. Of the two cultural engines; on the one hand integrative feminism driven by oxytocin and endo-opiate behaviors and on the other hand, male display-territory control driven by adrenaline analogs and stress states.

Oxytocin effects male sexual and bonding behaviors and choices. OT significantly increases during sexual arousal. At sexual climax, mean plasma OT rises about fivefold in men. The intensity of muscular contractions during orgasm in both men and women are highly correlated with OT plasma level (Gimpl et al. 2001). But oddly the reactions in both men and women are diminished by sex with multiple partners? It seems on the short term the reaction is reserved for pair bonded couples having repeated sex. *Further Reading-* (Physiological Reviews, Vol. 81, No. 2, April 2001, pp. 629-683 The Oxytocin Receptor System: Structure, Function, and Regulation Gerald Gimpl and Falk Fahrenholz).

Oxytocin related behaviors helped preserve mutual affection and cooperation in early human development between men and women. Women developed proactive sexual strategies to ensure security, and status. Out of those strategies may

47

have evolved the monthly sexual cycle, unique to homo sapiens. This constant male sexual contact triggered neuropeptide releases that encouraged sexual viability in women and kept men in a 'moderated behavioral state' via oxytocin interactions. Men became, in a sense, sexually domesticated by women. Men balanced between inner circle homeostatic reinforcing behaviors and environmental outer defensive behaviors to protect birthing strategies.

Part of these expanded sexual behaviors between men and women evolved to include a hidden signaling language related to rhythm. There is evidence that rhythmical instruments were being made 30,000 years ago, in the upper Paleolithic:

"Rasps or scrapers are well-known instruments, both from archaeological and ethnographic sources. Their distribution is almost world-wide. In its simplest form, the instrument consists of a notched stone, bone, shell or gourd, which is scrapped with a stick or other rigid object, the sound being increased in some instances by placing the instrument over a hole in the ground. It may be considered, together with the flute, as one of the earliest musical instruments known to man. A similar possible rasp is found at Riparo Mochi, Italy in deposits which are 35,000 years old". (Dirk Huyge,"Mousterian Skiffle? Note on a Middle Palaeolithic Engraved bone from Schulen, Belgium," Rock Art Research, 7(1990):2:125-133 p. 128-129) What if those instruments were used in music as a part of sexual communication?

Evidence of the effect of natural selection on rhythmic communication between men and women exists in today's studies of body language. One of the more interesting, is a study to understand the patterns of non-verbal synchronization in opposite sex encounters by Grammer, Kruck and Magnusson. They found that synchronization exists on a completely different level than expected between opposite sex encounters. They are "laden with highly complex unconscious non-verbal rhythmical movements over considerable time spans". The participants observed in their study were of a mean age of 18.5 years. What was found that If a female is interested in a male extraordinarily complex patterns of body language with a constant time structure emerge. This rhythmic structure of subconscious movements is an aspect of human courtship. If a female is interested in a male, she signals him with this hidden language to respond.

Their study proved that attempts to synchronize unconscious rhythmical body movements are initiated by the females so they can test compatibility with the males. If the female isn't interested there is no testing. Further, the number and complexity of the patterns is related to female interest in the male and the pleasure experienced in the situation, but not visa versa. These subtle rhythmical exchanges evolved through natural selection again allow us to speculate that rhythm played a large role in 'harmonizing' male and female behavior.

So men even today are being subconsciously invited into the higher level rhythmically based body language. They are being invited into the behavioral motif of feminine instinct. Music is a form of unconscious training in this body language exchange. Rhythmically based motor movements are learned when playing music. Rhythm and musical training involve repeating complex motor movements and committing them to memory. They become automatic, much like driving a car or riding a bike.

These automatic time-based movements become part of the broader non-verbal body language of the male musician or percussionist. Females 'read' these movements as sensual invitations or availability. Musicians become desirable sex partners not because of social status but because they are adept at this unconscious signaling. Anyone can give themselves this rhythmical aura without all the expensive social trappings just by learning rhythmical embedded cognition. It is why we see the renewed popularity in live drumming and dance. Men are searching for a renewed connection to inner circle tribal behaviors through music and rhythm.

Rhythm's Sexual Language

If the musical mind can directly converge with feminine dynamic mood shifts and hormonal changes then music dilutes gender differences. Music brings us together. Rhythmically based improvisational music embeds rhythmical signaling into our body language and verbal communication.

According to the embodied cognition hypothesis, thought patterns emerge from reinforced motor movements related to 'playing' a musical or rhythmical instrument. In this view, rhythm cognition includes physical sensation, visual clues from other players, and sonic reinforcement, without symbolic representation or thought process. Put simply, you play music with an empty mind and a body full of social signaling.

For musicians, a major part of musical skill involves the bodily coordination: "For musical performers, the difference between the musical experience and body motion disappears; the rhythmic motions of the performer and of the musical object are essentially one and the same. The knowledge of the musical style and its association with other players is embedded in the kinesthetic movement of the musician. The sense of self only gets in the way. (from <u>Microstructures of Feel, Macrostructures of Sound: Embodied Cognition in West African and African American Music</u> By Vijay S. Lyer)

Musicians then are used to conforming their kinesthetic self with other musicians or dancers. They can unconsciously drop into the complex rhythmical body language signaling from interested females with ease. They easily become part of the feminine rhythmical dialogue hidden in body language. In fact, recent scientific studies seem to suggest that music may have been a human trait long before complex spoken language as a component for seduction and mating.

We were mere hunters and gatherers when music developed. Bone flutes from man's hunting and gathering period, over thirty thousand years old, have been found in Paleolithic sights in Europe. There are researchers that think music as courtship came before language in humans. Music comprehension uses areas of the brain associated with early brain development in children. It is why children's learning skills are enhanced by musical listening and learning.

Bjørn Grinde in an article that was first published in 2000 in ©Nordic Journal of Music Therapy contends that Individuals which can produce any kind of primitive song may be reproductively more successful through sexual selection. Moreover, the group of singing and dancing individuals, whatever the genetic make-up of the individuals, may become more successful because of the increased group identity awareness which makes its members cooperate more efficiently. Even Darwin suggested a possible evolutionary connection between language and music in his book. ("Descent of Man". 1998)

Ashe as Ancient Knowledge

Male musicians have been historically favored as sex partners by women. The lore of musical sexual prowess comes from many distant cultures and parts of the world with evidence that rhythm and tone instruments have evolved for over 30,000 years.

One myth of understanding of the male musical contribution to feminine instinct in this century is the African myth of Legba. Legba's myth is embedded in the Afro-American musical tradition handed down by oral teaching and rhythmical training related to our tribal relationship to music. Legba's myth is that of stimulator of sexual polymorphism and homeostasis that is represented by his irresistible talents at seduction.

The lore of Legba in African rhythmical culture is a historical example of the rhythmical shaman that we model contemporary 'Rock' or 'Hip-Hop' sensuality on. Legba is considered the gatekeeper, the door opener into the world of synchronicity and mystical love. To Legba, rhythm and male sexuality are inseparable. The slang word "Mojo" is derived from this blending. Mojo is rhythmically interlinked with homeostasis.

Leslie Desmangles, in T he Faces of the Gods describes Legba: " Legba is the patron of the universe, the link between the Godhead and the universe, the umbilical cord that connects the

53

universe to its origin. Bondye fashioned the universe, Legba has nurtured it, fostered its growth, and has sustained it. It is He who is invoked in matters related to sex."

Leslie's book concentrates on how easy it was for African Drumming religions to absorb Christianity into their rhythmical, integrative context. Religious ideology is transparent to the effects of musical consciousness. Ideologies linguistic trappings hold little power over the more primal forceful auditory/kinesthetic mind/body knowledge of African music. Legba represents rhythmical integration and hormonal balance. Legba's myths acknowledge the paradigm of feminine homeostasis.

White culture banned the drums in the Southern plantations and anthropomorphized Legba into the Devil. But, Legba represents the antithesis of the Devil's chaos. The Devil embraces chaos and fear. Legba represents rhythmical harmony and temporal perfection, spiritual connection, hormonal homeostasis, and connection to nature. Legba represents the male/female inner circle hormonal complex of 30,000 years of evolution. Legba represents cohesion and synergy, not anarchism.

Legba's myth of sexual prowess is related to complete oneness with the temporal and rhythmic experience. The myth assumes that sexual timing is controlled by the feminine and men serve that timing with rhythmical awareness. With extensive rhythmic training, the myth says you 'take Legba in your head'. This is exactly a description of embedded cognition of rock musicians and utilization of bilateral thinking. Once this style of thought process is part of your consciousness and 'Legba' is in 'your head', you are given a special way of looking at things. This rhythmical awareness gained through the mastery of rhythm is called in the African Yoruba dialect: "Ashae". Among the Yoruba of Africa this subtlety is the essence of understanding the "supreme deity": The supreme deity is called among the Yoruba; Olorun master of the skies. Olorun is nether male or female but a vital force. Olorun is the supreme quintessence of "Ashae."

"Ashe" is seeing everything holistically. 'Ashae' is the act of seeing into the synergy of the instant. The world dynamic becomes rhythmically transparent. It is rhythmic determinism. To have "Ashae" is to be rhythmically on time or 'cool' to your surroundings. You do not understand "Ashe" until you become it. Ashae recognizes releasing bound sexual tension moving towards homeostasis and ending rhythmical discord. Legba's actions relate to releasing something that is out of rhythm with its true nature. 'Ashae' is the synergy Legba is living within. It is with this sub rosa sensibility of the African myths of 'Legba' and 'Ashae' that Afro-American music revitalized and sexualized popular American music. The African drummer priest is related to the blues player, jazz musician, Hip-Hop artist of today. And within these musical movements is the implicit understanding of the seductive qualities of rhythm.

Krishna's Flute

In a Hindu account of the mythical deity Krishna, polymorphic diffuse sexuality related to oxytocin enhancement is further connected to sensual naturalism where the natural world participates in his flute magic. Krishna is the supreme musical Godhead. In this mythical story written by Serial Visvanatha in 1685 the tale of Krishna's rhythmical seduction is accounted for. Here Krishna seduces not only the Women playing in the water but seduces nature itself:

"Krishna and the gopis began to slap the water with their hands, playing nice rhythms and music. When this sound, that defeated the rumbling of the clouds, echoed on the shore of the kunda the chataka birds began to wander around, the peacocks began to dance like mad, with their tail feathers spread out, singing, 'ke ka', and Monkey began to slap his armpits and danced along with them, exclaiming his 'hee hee!' When the trees on the shore of the kunda heard this, they showered streams of honey into the water as tears of love and the honeybees praised them".

Here we feel the power of male musical awareness imbued with mystical awareness of nature. Krishna is seducing us with music. His music seduces nature also. Krishna personifies a musical male sexual God. He is an archetype, a model of sexual expression, connection with nature, mystical awareness to emulate. This is a love triangle between Krishna, Radha, and Nature. Nature responds as a lover would succumb to Krishna's deep awareness of music.

"The Hindu god Krishna, the avatar of Vishnu, is at once great god of the universe and shepherd boy beloved of all the shepherd women. His flute made them dance with abandon. The music of Krishna's pipe is Eros freed from the bounds of society, its rules, laws, restrictions, morality. It is the love of the human soul unsullied even by language. Logos--words, reason-- release their customary grip and let the soul soar on wings that logic and science cannot know. By means of his flute, Krishna fills himself and the universe with bliss. He distracts everyone and everything from normal activity and enchants them to revel in ecstasy. His flute sends shudders of delight to the very foundations of the world.

Natural laws fall away as rocks and trees respond to his call and stars wander from their courses. The sound of his flute puts an abrupt end to man's mechanical, habitual activity as well as to the predictable movements of nature. His music explodes upon the world and society insisting that all else be forgotten. It is time, it proclaims, to join in his symphony of joy, to frolic in the forest, to scamper in play, to realize every dream that one has ever dreamed in his world of infinite possibility.

Overtones

An ancient bone flute segment, estimated at about 43,000 up to 82,000 years old, was found recently at an early man campsite by Dr. Ivan Turk, a paleontologist at the Slovenian Academy of Sciences in Ljubljana. It's confirmed age makes it the oldest known musical instrument. The sound holes suggest a harmonic vibratory relationship.

Archaeologists have also found in China more than thirty 9000-year-old flutes all made from the wing bone of the red-crowned crane and carved with five to seven holes. These instruments were delicate and highly evolved, measuring about 20 centimeters in length and one and a half centimeters in width. Evidence of the harmonic relationship of the sound holes in them is well documented.

There is great significance in these harmonic flute finds. 'Harmonic' overtones are contained in any created musical note and in nature. The overtones of any one note all add up to its major chord. The most audible overtones of a tonic or keynote all have simple ratios. In fact these three notes are present in virtually every musical scale known on earth. If you write out the overtones of these three notes and string out the three most audible ones of each within the span of an octave, you will get the major scale.

'Harmonic' tones from these early flutes, if two or more played at the same time, created rhythms caused by interference patterns effecting alpha and theta brain wave states associated with meditation. Interference patterns between two different tones create secondary beats of a lower frequency. Theta and Alpha brain wave patterns that are associated with relaxation and meditation are below the sound threshold of the human ear, about 10 to 30 beats per second." (LANE, J. D., S. J. KASIAN, J. E. OWENS AND G. R. MARSH. Binaural auditory beats affect vigilance performance and mood. PHYSIOL BEHAV 63(2) 249 252, 1998.)

In 1839 H. W. Dove, a German musical experimenter, discovered the auditory effect of binaural beats (Oster, 1973). He found that when two different frequencies of sound were presented, one to each ear, a third frequency equal to the difference between the two frequencies was perceived.

This third, beat is the result of the interaction of the two primary tones within the auditory brainstem. For example, if a pure tone with a frequency of 400 Hz is presented to one ear and a second tone of 410 Hz is presented to the other ear, a third beat with a frequency of 10 Hz will also be heard because of the interaction of the two frequencies. In a primitive setting if more than one flute was being played, this third tone that was heard could have taken on religious significance.

These ghostlike beats can be generated at frequencies below 40 Hz and may be used to entrain electrical rhythms of the brain to vibrate at the same frequency through the new frequency.

Alpha and Theta brain waves range of the electrical rhythms of the human cortex go from 0 Hz to about 40 Hz. Since humans have an auditory range of 20 to 20,000 Hz, it is not possible to directly entrain cortical rhythms below 20 Hz with pure tones. However, the phenomenon of beats from overtones, an auditory brainstem response, allows the entrainment of frequencies below 30 Hz through the interaction of pure harmonic tones. We experience this effect as an emotional affinity to certain cords or musical scales that sound 'sweet' rather than discordant.

Thirty thousand years ago something happened in an evolutionary instant with our early ancestors. Harmonics and rhythm became part of early man's life. It was then that symbolic art materialized. Harmonic flutes and symbolic art evolved at the same time. Early man was experimenting with the power of music to enhance emotional states associated with symbolic art.

Iconic Male Display

It was during this time, in the Upper Paleolithic, that the early Venus 'iconic' figures appeared throughout Europe and Russia. Perhaps, this was the first quantum leap in supporting feminine homeostasis using music and iconography. We can only guess. The appearance of music and Goddess iconography parallels a rapid European population expansion of homo sapiens that has been described by anthropologists as having been static for 75,000 years before these technologies are evidenced. A stable expansion of humanity continued since their introduction suggesting that musical relaxation and musical sexuality triggered greater fertility and hormonal balance, and sense of safety.

In the last twenty years of his life, Marshall McLuhan, the famous anthropologist, and media expert published a series of books that established his reputation as a world- renowned communications theorist and the pre-eminent seer of the modern age. It was McLuhan who coined the phrases "The medium is the message." and "The global village".

McLuhan predicted in 1964 that electronic communication would cause a shift in the way we assimilate ideas. He predicted that logical argument and rational deduction would be displaced by 'spin' and image management. He said that territory and culture would be assimilated and blended by instant communication worldwide. And he understood the return to 'iconic' myth and instinctually of our ancestors 30,000 years ago. He described and coined the term "electronic village".

Now forty years later we live in the reality of his projections. Ideas and issues are battled over with images and sound bites. Ideas are sown and sold by musical tone, rhythm, and iconography in a television or internet instant. Ideas are absorbed by our instinctual reactions to carefully crafted multi-sensory dramas.

All the old territorial male polemic institutions of the written word are buried in the endless chatter of image and musical regulation of instinct. Writing favored male instinct by being a medium that supported static intellectual and physical domain. Instant communication is blurring ideologies and inflicting the intellectual male paragon to an endless barrage of feminine images and musical embodiment of the feminine instinctual dynamic. Even the most ardent critics of the music/sex revolution admit to its overwhelming presence.

In "Technoply, The Surrender of Culture to Technology", By Neil Postman, Mr. Postman contends that "the uncontrolled growth of technology destroys our humanity. It creates a culture without moral foundation and reorders our fundamental assumptions about the world at large. New technologies alter our understanding of what is real, "which is another way of saying that embedded in every tool is an ideological bias, a predisposition to construct the world as one thing rather than another."

One of the most ominous consequences of "Technopoly", according to Postman, is the explosion of context-free information. "The milieu in which "Technopoly" flourishes is one in which the tie between information and human purpose has been severed, i.e., information appears indiscriminately, directed at no one in particular, in enormous volume and at high speeds, and disconnected from theory, meaning, or purpose." The "information glut" leads to the breakdown of a coherent cultural narrative, he argues, for without a meaningful context, information is not only useless, but potentially dangerous. He cites the old saying that, to a man with a hammer, everything looks like a nail, and therefore, "to a man with a computer, everything looks like data."

Postman sees the contextual and narrative ideas of governance, religion, morality, and education being eroded by instant communication, imagery, and manipulation of instinct.

In the new medium of communication, you are subjected to instant manipulation of your basic instincts. Electronic visual and auditory 'spin' 'streams' our male and female instinctual behaviors in equal and overwhelming amounts. Moral context and moral narrative of male territoriality of the feminine is lost to a mosaic of visual and auditory juxtaposition of music and sensual broadcasting of the more akin to feminine instinct.

That could be why government and religion seem so ineffectual and off target about issues that have to do with sensuality and sexual choice. Even feminism cannot be wholly an intellectual and static association of ideas. Feminism has languished in its own narrative, while the 'iconic' and musical youth culture redefines feminine/masculine behavior within the context of new communication mediums. Music and image bring with it its own ethos.

Women experience complex kinesthetic and rhythmical 'proto-sexual' relationships with other women to enhance networked feminine homeostasis. Quite often mistaken for lesbianism by men, scientific evidence shows oxytocin enhancement and endorphin enhancement are related to tactile and kinesthetic cooperation as women reach toward the mutual goal of shared hormonal balance. Studies show how this behavior causes improved bioregulation and immunity related to reproductive success.

Proto-sexual communication in dance may not be what it appears to be to the casual male observer.

Sexually aroused males may comprehend seemingly sexual interactions between women from their instinctual context of threat to territory and competition missing totally the instinctual homeostatic signals between women.

Madison Avenue gets it. Homeostasis is expressed in calming multimedia imagery associated with tactile communication, relaxation, and emotionally releasing body movement. Modern feminine sensual iconography constantly suggests sexual polymorphism as symbol for higher 'comfort' levels associated with balanced hormonal dynamics instead of goal oriented sexual needs of males. Endorphin, oxytocin, and testosterone increase, nitrogen oxide stimulation, and Alpha brain wave enhancements related to repetitive sound patterns (music), enhance emotion and bioregulation in females.

Feminine instinctual 'ideology' is based on a physical response embedded in technology. As mediums of communication affect instinct they are reflected in cultural 'normalization' of gender related goals. Musical reproduction, and the repetition of multimedia advertising has had direct role in normalizing feminine biological synergy. The mediums reinforce feminine instinctual clues.

Cross Rhythms at the Crossroads

Voodoo in the 1800's was a fusion of African drumming religions that blended together because of the cultural displacement of black slaves. It was a mix of drumming and dance religions from many parts of Africa. The drumming and dance religions that became Voodoo were dominated by the Fon and Dohemy cultures of West Africa. In both 1791 and 1804, a series of slave revolts rocked Haiti. The revolts were based around the practice of Vodun and they ended with the French being expulsed from the island. The African slave drumming rituals were used to war against the French overlords.

The French white captors had assumed their superiority. But polyrhythmic drumming, long periods of dancing, and iconic re-enactments of success in overcoming the French drove the strong black slaves into a frenzy. Rhythm played a major part in these rituals. The strong background groove and polyrhythmic counterpoints induced a mental clarity and deep conviction for the task before them. The French were no match for the hypnotic power of rhythm.

The slaves, driven by these drumming rituals, would then go out and slaughter their French masters. It became such a problem that the French quit Haiti. But many of the French were able to escape to New Orleans and many of them brought their slaves with them. The African drumming religions in Haiti were a vital mix of many drumming rites carried over from Africa. The slaves who revolted were called "Maroons" hence the term "Marooned" came into our vocabulary.

Rebellious imported slaves continued to drum and dance in the bayous of Louisiana. In 1817 the New Orleans Municipal Council passed a resolution forbidding blacks to gather for dancing or any other purpose except on Sundays and only in places designated by the mayor. The accepted spot was Congo Square on North Rampart Street, now called Beauregard Square. Slaves danced and drummed in Congo Square overtly worshipping their gods while the whites looked on.

Many slaves were baptized into the Catholic church and later, the use of these Catholic icons would play a major role in their new world religion of Voodoo. Catholicism and Voodoo became intermingled. Soon after the introduction of the African slaves to New Orleans, Voodoo began to play a major part in the lives of the general populace.

The crossbreeding of Catholicism and drumming culture influenced the white population as well. The whites feared voodoo but at the same time accepted its Catholic iconography and ritual. But more importantly, the white plutocracy was attracted to it because of its open sexuality, sexualized private rituals, and secret orgies that the whites often participated in. The white male aristocracy in New Orleans took advantage and their slaves sexual prowess and connection with rhythm.

In New Orleans a blending of cultures and races started contemporary musical sexuality based on the rhythms and lore of the African drumming cultures of immigrant slaves. The French freed any second-generation slave by law. Many of these female slaves were women of mixed race, a mixture of both black and white parents. The most notorious of these women was Marie Laveau the Voodoo Priestess of New Orleans.

Marie Laveau was born in New Orleans in 1794 and was considered a free woman of color because of

French law. Marie took up employment as a hairdresser catering to the wealthy white and Creole women of New Orleans. All the while she was learning the secrets of Voodoo, the dancing, the drum rhythms, the ceremonies, the pantheon of deities, and foremost the sexuality. Her job put her ear close to the secrets of the social life of New Orleans.

For her to claim the title of "Mambo" of the New Orleans, she had to have the pedigree of her connection to the hypnotic rhythms and rituals derived from Haitian slaves. She would have to hold together a tight circle of drummers as her assistants. She would have to strike fear in her enemies and nurture her aspirants. She would have learned to barter and arrange sexual liaisons. She herself would manipulate her white overseers by inciting them into erotic encounters with sexually adept young black women. She would use the secrets told to her as a hairdresser to expand her influence. She would have to out dance her rivals and practice magic against them. She would have to appear subservient while manipulating her white benefactors. All of this was an outstanding feat for an illegitimate black girl with no status. Iconography, vision, and rhythms established that status for her.

Marie was queen. Marie made so much happen in New Orleans because of her talents. She is believed to be responsible for the open music in Conga Square. Black drumming culture and musical sensibility stuck its foot in the American door. The worship of the spontaneous Gods and Goddesses of West African spiritual drumming cultures became music that developed into the improvisational "cool" musical styles coming out of New Orleans. Styles like, second line, blues, be-bop, rhythm and blues, jazz, rock and roll, reggae, ska, rap, and hip-hop owe their origins to the drumming in Congo Square.

American music became Afro-American music. Much of the early music by blacks contained improvisation. Rhythmic improvisation predominated in African Religious music. And instead of Christianity absorbing the black music something else happened. Christian music became Africanized. The preachers call and chorus banter echoed the drumming and dancing and vocalizations of African ancestors. Blacks may have come here naked and beaten but their musical spirit engulfed white America. Sex and music, rhythm, and spontaneity, seduced the Victorian mindset.

But in America unlike Brazil, Cuba, Santo Domingo, and the West Indies, the drumming religions died here. Blacks owned the music but lost the spiritual tools of the master drumming societies of their African homeland by suppression and white propaganda.

One of the deities was "Legba," the African keeper of the "crossroads". In African ritual Legba is the gatekeeper. He is the cross rhythms that induce hypnotic trance, lucid dreaming, and emotional catharsis. Legba lets you into the world of perfect timing in the metaphysical now.

To whites, Legba was the Devil. The cross rhythms became the crossroads. A meeting place for a Faustian pact with the devil instead of an opening into higher consciousness. African rhythmical shamanism and sense of contact with nature was

68

lost in the Christian dialogue about Devil Worship among their white masters.

With the dialogue forfeited, secret knowledge of sexual healing with rhythm and the neurological enhancements of music were twisted into a secular side show of wantonness and depravity. This secularism has left us with erotic adventurism and materialism of today's Hip-Hop and Rock and Roll. Legba's legacy of live musical support of dance has been lost against the din of recorded and machine-driven simple 4/4 rhythms.

Imagine an African drummer priest drawing signs in the dust surrounded by a din of tribal music. A circle of dancers look on moving receptively. Our journey starts here amid the noise of multiple drummers and expressive dancing. In West African tribal drumming and dance, the tribal musical event is viewed as a crossing point between the individual and the tribe for renewal and unification. The tribal dancer is seen not as a fixed personality but as a tribal variable in constant state of change. The dance is ever changing in the moment, assuming various roles sympathetic to the steady state of tribal survival and cultural history. The musical events are cathartic points of emotional cohesion and tribal balance. **The cross-rhythms are the crossroads.**

In Western scientific thinking we reflect on pieces of the whole. We observe and manipulate parts of the whole in nature. Conversely tribal dance cultures dwell on our oneness with all things by entering the source of rhythm intrinsic to everything. Our black ancestors developed methods for accessing and becoming one with the singular force nature in all things through music.

These unifying experiences were opened by the rhythms. Live rhythmical grooves connect a group of players with something beyond. In the discipline of the players, they interact with instantaneous subconscious perfection. The rhythms act to fold life and meaning upon itself into a transparency of interrelatedness. Man intersected with nature in an integrative instant. We wouldn't know these experiences from our cultural vantage point. We lack the "cool" or "hipness" or "Ashe" to experience them.

Priest and Priestess were both revered, passing on subtle ancient wisdom on the nature of time, rhythm and the power of the rhythmic "crossroads". Sex was atmospheric here, engrossing everyone's attention through rhythm and dance. The priestess mated with the Gods. She articulated her power and position in the community through divine understanding and her sensual expressiveness.

African lore is filled with the power of the priestess. As Marie Leveau maneuvered among the high society with her secret drumming and dance teachings, she was setting the stage for the acceptance of African music and sensibility in America. Our very sensual freedom as women here in America owes much to the African experience. Music and our own sensual drives delivered us from our Victorian male dominated angst. We copied black women. We copied their dances. In Africa many social institutions were male dominated but fear and seduction tempered the patriarchy. The secret feminine priesthoods of Africa wielded power from within. We were learning to do the same through Africanized music. It made us feel the power of our sexuality.

Music and Polymorphic Release

The rhythms of our physical functions are directly affected by our ability to experience and emotionally direct pleasure. Pleasure sets our inner clock of hormones, digestive functions, sexual cycles, and moods. Music, pleasure and maximized body rhythms complement each other and reinforce each other. We can experience undifferentiated pleasure and really understand the transmutable nature of sexuality through music.

Beyond our Western preoccupation with specific genital sexual sensation or specific sexual technique, are the more subtle elements of connecting to rhythm and timing in feminine sexual experience. The more we are 'in tune' or 'on time' with our partner's sensations, the deeper and more primal the experience becomes. Music breaks down our egoistic sexual preoccupations.

As we learn rhythm, movement, and timing, in the kinesthesia of musical memory, these elements become as important as the physical act of sex stimulation. Our timing and attention evolve out of our complex cellular identity. Nothing personal diverts us from our expressive union. Music becomes our sexual language.

Developed musical understanding attunes us with our primal desire to nurture and integrate. To nurture and integrate is the basic biological imperative of feminine consciousness. Integration is not a feminine intellectual concept. It is a basic physiological experience and a medium of communication that women have long held in their genetic code. It cannot be escaped. The whole body and select emotional states play a large role in experiencing pleasure. Sound, movement, and emotional catharsis can spontaneously induce orgasmic states. In the following account from Egypt around 1920 we get a glimpse of the secretive dances of the Middle East.

"It seemed to have a magic effect, for their pervious frenzy had been cold compared with the mad fury which now possessed them. .... Their gestures and cries were frantic...

Sometimes they bent their bodies back till they formed a writhing and vibrating bow, resting on the ground by the heels and the back of the head whist the muscles of their bodies carried on the dance with unbelievable contortions many of the women in bacchanalian frenzy were pulling from their bosoms, they proceeded to sing songs which were erotic, in keeping , their dancing became indecent"(McPhearson, 1920.)

Among the Voi tribe in Africa also, such experiences were be found as described in this account:

"A woman could be lead up close to the drums, and then her whole body would jerk and show orgasmic reactions to the drumming. And the drummers themselves seemed to be trying to produce the maximum effect in the particular participant in

front of them" (Anon. Account from among the Voi tribe in Kenya)

Secretly musical sexuality was practiced in the American South. Music and sex married and grew up together in the young and resourceful American experience enhanced by popular acceptance of secular forms of musical ritual and that enhanced sensuality denied by the Victorian era.

Music itself creates a cultural support system where women are given room to experience sexual feelings in a safe environment. Using kinesthetic motor conditioning and rhythmic meditation, women find sensual resonance with music because of their biological imperative. Women find ways to create positive emotional change through music.

Sexualized emotional release is blended with music. Anyone has a ypung daughter knows female children are living in a world of music and lyrical repetition. Often young girls will memorize and repeat lyrics to songs over and over never tiring of the process. When they get together, they will sing the lyrics in unison. The radio is always on. This cultural phenomenon is instinctually based communication to reinforce feminine communal homeostasis.

The iconic male musician taps into this instinctual drive often without direct knowledge of its existence. One of the first persons to intellectually understand this drive was the founder of modern hypnotism Mesmer, where the word Mesmerizing comes from.

Mesmer's Buckets

Franz Mesmer was the founder of modern hypnotism. Franz Mesmer was forced to leave France around 1785 because of the agitation of high society over his electromagnetism 'techniques' for his-female oriented parlor séances that became the rage of French high society. Mesmer claimed to use magnetism to 'cure' his female patents. His seances were performed using several parlor tricks and a dramatic environment that consisted of a darkened room with astrological symbols and lavish and strange furnishings. The strangest was a baquet.

In a medical museum in Lyon there is a strange tub-like object constructed of oak and decorated with lengths of ornately woven rope. About six inches in from the rim, eight evenly spaced iron rods sprout up from a highly polished lid. In the eighteenth century, a group of patients would sit or stand around this device in such a way as to press the afflicted areas of their bodies against these moveable metal wishbones and, bound to the instrument by the ropes, would link fingers to complete an "electric" circuit. On the inside the eight protruding rods were inserted into eight cylinders, each of which had a powerful magnet at its base. The tub still contains two layers of sixteen bottles, arranged in a radial pattern on a bed of crushed glass, pounded sulfur, and iron filings; watermarks indicate that the vat would also have been filled to the brim with magnetized water. Such an elaborate device would indicate that Mesmer thought

74

the device was important and not an artifact of parlor tricks.

The *baquet* was essentially a gigantic bucket, a huge Leyden jar supposedly charged by the animal magnetism emanating from Mesmer's own person. Mesmer believed that animal magnetism "could be stored up and concentrated, like an electric fluid and that with the aid of the magnetic reservoir in his therapeutic prop he could distribute the full force of his own peculiar "vital fire" to a burgeoning clientele. The device had several iron hooks that you would hold onto while locking hands with the person next to you. Mesmer would come and dramatically touch his clients. Especially touching the 'lower abdomen' of his female clients while they were attached to his device. Mesmer was using rhythm and theatrics to the point where his all women séance would end in a mutual sexualized swoon. The report stated:

"The crisis continues, however, and the eye is obscured, an unequivocal sign of the complete disorder of the senses, the eyelids become moist, the respiration is short and interrupted, the chest heaves rapidly, convulsions set in, and either the limbs or the whole body is agitated by sudden movements. In lively and sensitive women this last stage, which terminates the sweetest emotion, is often a convulsion: To this condition there succeeded languor, prostration, and a sort of slumber of the senses." from a report commissioned by Luis the XVI.

Music and rhythm were supplied to the experience by an invention of Benjamin Franklin. It was called a glass harmonica. It consisted of twenty bowls inserted within each other on a long rod. The rod would rotate, and the player would run wet fingers on the edge of the individual bowls. This created a haunting sound with many overtones from adjacent bowls. The stage was set. Mesmer grew to immense popularity.

Luis the XVI of France prepared a special private report for himself in addition to a watered-down version publicly published. Issued in 1784, the scathing report finally resulted in Mesmer having to leave France as a charlatan. He first settled at Spa in Belgium, where he established a free mesmerism clinic, and then went to Constance in Germany. The King of Prussia invited him to practice in Berlin, but he refused. However, a Chair of Mesmerism was established at the Berlin Academy and a hospital devoted solely to mesmerism was founded there.

Meanwhile in France the popularity for his devices grew. Mesmer also initiated a training program, establishing a Society of Universal Harmony whose members paid handsomely to be initiated into the mysteries of his esoteric technique. Nicolas Bergasse, the Society's first member, wrote an instruction manual, which was only decipherable with a key of cabbalistic signs. On the eve of the French Revolution, the Society had 430 graduates, with thriving satellite organizations in every major French city. There were up to 6,000 unsanctioned Mesmerists operated in and around Paris alone in 1785.

The Commission was hinting that attacks of mesmeric excitement leading to trance and collapse were polymorphous (diffuse) female orgasms. The private report ended with the warning that there was nothing to prevent the convulsions from becoming habitual in certain patients, or from producing an epidemic earlier reported in convents. The Commission even suggested that the damage caused to patients by mesmeric treatment might be 'transmitted to future generations', and they felt that there might be an injurious effect on public morals. These were polymorphic sexual experiences that went beyond genital stimulation.

"Women were in the majority and the first crisis that occurred was contagious. **It took two or three hours to establish such a crisis** *(integrative orgasmic release). The crisis is characterized by involuntary movement, cries, tears, and laughter followed by a state of stupor or languor." (Binet and Fere. 1860)*

Mesmer observed that women were easier to hypnotize. Is this caused by feminine sensory bias towards their linguistic, tactile, and auditory integration? What Mesmer did not realize was the powerful role rhythm played in his parlor experiences. The swooning experiences of Mesmer's Victorian groups closely resembled more primitive tribal dance rituals. These were proto-sexual and polymorphic sexual experiences. They had phases like a sexual experience but without any genital direct stimulation but might also have included orgasm. The experience was integrated into the social setting of Victorian Europe. What Mesmer intuited was a sense of timing and its delicate relationship with sensation supported by his flare for dramatic props, actions and rhythmical speech.

Like Marie Laveaux, Mesmer was using drama, rhythm and suggestive touch to trigger his female clients polymorphic sexual reaction. Rhythmical sexual experiences well up from within and spill over into the conscious from the unconscious without any direct sexual stimulation. This happens because of alterations in the limbic system associated with hormonal and neurotransmitter changes setting up the body for experiencing diffuse orgasm. An Indian Vedic holy woman, "Anandamaya Ma" describes this experience of diffuse, non- specific sensual orgasm in her teachings:

"When something is boiled in a closed vessel, there comes a stage when the vapor will push up the lid and, unless force is used, the vessel cannot be kept covered any more. In a similar manner, when, while being engaged in Japa or some other spiritual exercise a wave of ecstatic emotion surges up from within, it becomes difficult to check it. It emerges from deep within and expresses itself outwardly." *Anandamayi Ma- Dacca, India (From: Bhaiji. 1973)*

Timing is Everything

Feminine sexuality is diffuse. It depends outwardly on time of the month, setting, sense of safety, physical wellbeing, warmth, lighting, etc. It is also dependent inwardly; on rhythm, fantasy, relaxation and the subtle relationship between fantasy and physical sensation.

Sensation rides rhythm. Rhythm with drums or hypnosis becomes a circle of safety in dreamy sensual acceptance and release. It allows a woman to feel completely connected to physical sensation. Rhythm is a grounding or landscape for the integration of mind and body. Inside rhythm, sexuality and orgasm integrate into dreamlike visionary experiences. In Kundalini yoga, a sensual form of yogic practice, there is use of rhythmic chanting and body movements. A woman Kundalini priestess describes outward visible effects of these integrative experiences:

"The Goddess may be seen as a lightning flash or chain of lights shaking or trembling of the body, hair standing on end, involuntary deep breathing, laughing, weeping, stammering, fearful visions, fixation of sight, stopping of breath, revolving eyeballs, vibrations in the spinal cord, convulsions, waves of bliss, hearing mantras, the body falling on the floor, .jerking and tossing of the body, intoxication, energy and endurance, visions of deities, and magical powers."(Swami Vishnu Tirtha, Devatma Shakti)

Through rhythm and integrative sensation, a woman transcends into an altered reality. There is an unfolding of self that overrides ordinary consciousness. By being totally absorbed into the present rhythm takes on a new dimension. It is a resonant point in personal time where we enter our past, present, and future selves. We pass through a 'crossing point' of our many self-expressions and transform into a new person. No doubt it is why there is an "X" in sex. And adult material is described as XXX. Rhythm is the grounding and safety medium for sexual transformation. The X is the crossing or mixing of integrated sensations and feelings that sex causes.

Rhythm and Metaphor

In various sensual/musical rituals social support is held through group meditation on metaphor. Physiological support is held by rhythmic repetition and rhythmic sensual movement. Metaphor contains for each person an image and emotional tone that is psychically ridden to sexual release. Each culture embraces a different set of metaphors, navigating the sexual celebrant selflessly into subconscious unity with the cultural support system created for their positive experience. In the past, live music has paid an important part in this kind musical release.

In our secular culture, rock musicians or DJ's are the metaphor or iconic symbol. You could call them personality cults, but the musicians or DJ's in contemporary long rhythmical group settings are valid metaphors for sexual reckoning through rhythm. With most Women there is little chance they could sexually experience an adored musician. For the few it's a sexual challenge. But the real sensual message is in the metaphor and the music itself. Metaphor and music are guides to undifferentiated pleasure and sexual release

Ancient musical navigators have guided experiences of our distant ancestors by directing thought and emotion towards the center of music, the dance and cultural support. Rhythm and synchronous sensation over long periods of time draw us to a point where we become the metaphor itself. We are captivated by the support of those with us. The respect and reverences that are held for the deities, power animals, gods, goddesses, and rock musicians give us a social setting that validates diffuse sensual experience inside music.

Women express their sexuality in a profoundly integrated way. Their genetically encoded sensory bias integrates physical sensations, emotional context, movement, and rhythm to create ecstasy. The dancer can experience overwhelming undifferentiated love, overwhelming pleasure, and deep mystical oneness with their metaphorical connection. This often happens without direct physical contact or specific sexual stimulation. It only happens with the continuing practice of the methods necessary to trigger such states. Body positive cultures have a common line of experiences and practices that support integrative sexual states. Besides the examples of Marie Leaveau's voodoo Christian saints and Mesmer's electromagnetic forces, there are other metaphors that can complement the physical changes induced by rhythm and long dancing sessions.

Erzuli

From West African improvisational drumming cultures, the percussive sexual African Goddess metaphor of Erzuli secretly took hold in the in the Americas. The metaphor of the water Goddesses of sexual love and psychic union were transplanted here.   Often Erzuli hid behind more outspoken, outrageous, and angry Gods disturbed by the injustice of slavery. But She too was important to the nuances of African musical form in the Americas. The secret arts of African sex magic were carried on in the Voodoo of Haiti and morphed into today's thriving black music culture.

Erzuli is one of the River Goddesses of West Africa as was Oshun- from the Yoruba, and Aziri- from the Fon tribes. In Haitian Voodoo, Erzuli is the rhythmic Goddess of love. In Haiti She is called a "Loa". When possessed by her you are called a "cheval" or horse. She rides you, guiding your actions.

Outside the town of Ville-Bonheur in the mountains of Haiti are two waterfalls. It is said that to be bathed in the falls one will become blessed by Erzuli and healed. Pilgrims tie blue and pink cloth girdles around their waists and remove them when they reach the falls. Ritualistically they fasten them around the neighboring trees.

Services to Erzuli are very private. Whites did not know of them until dance forms to her were embraced by the Bohemian dance community of the early twentieth century. To be invited to such a service was a privilege

Erzuli is called with her specific drum rhythms. On the ceremonial floor food gifts honor her. A ground painting is drawn to call Her. The Mambo (Priestess) and the Houngan (Priest) set the rhythms and the songs to Her. Women dance gracefully to Her. The circle of support, movement, song cycle, and rhythms continue deep into the night, until Erzuli "mounts" her "Cheval" or "Horse" (is channeled by a parishioner).

The dancer becomes her. Erzuli chooses how her "Cheval" is to be affected. Erzuli channels through her aspirant's Sensuality. Haitian's have identified Erzuli with the Virgin Mary. She is "Pure" in a different sense of the word from the Christian Mother. To assert Erzuli's virginity is to say she is untouched by the corruptions of the living. Voodooists do not see her promiscuity as a sign of corruption. For a devotee to call Erzuli a "virgin" is to say that She is of another world, another reality. So, if you become sexually expressive honoring Erzuli there is no moral condemnation. You are considered touched by her spirit. That sexual expression is outside the realm of judgment and ownership. Again, long rhythms and dances to Erzuli trigger altered states of complex endo-neuromodulation. The body state precludes the metaphorical transformation.

Erzuli's purity is in the perfection of her rhythmical beauty and her purity as a Goddess, not in her virginity or in her sexual abstinence. Sex is part of experiencing Her. She makes love to the "Loas" and her earthly consorts bringing them closer together. At the heart of Her experience is rhythm, timing, and emotional tone lays the groundwork for feminine erotic release.

Her "Mystery" is *the sweet rain* of synchronism's that befalls those who hold her worship close to their hearts. Synchronism is driven by life beyond the ego. The black magic love of Western popular song indirectly praises Her. The" black magic woman" of Western popular music is Erzuli's woman who knows perfect timing. She is the priestess who is in the right place at the right time with love. American history has evaded this power granted to African American women

Erzuli's image and symbols are revered in almost every home in Haiti. She has many names and many moods, from the tragically jealous "Erzuli Rouge" to the nurturing "Erzuli Freda". They all come alive in the dance and the drums.

Erzuli is a metaphorical navigator used for personal transcendence inside the drum rhythms. Her worship joins sex with music in the women that experience Her. She allows love to transcend the ordinary. The power of mystical cross rhythms and lore of the African "crossroads" includes Erzuli's worship. Again we find yet another metaphor and group dynamic with long rhythm and dance cycles for parapsychological expression.

Shakti's Rhythmical Triggers

Halfway across the world in Vedic culture there is Tantra. Although most Yogi's limit sensation to assuage karmic expression on the world. There are some adepts that use sex as a method of opening the chakras. The aim of Tantra is to expand awareness in all states of consciousness, whether a waking state, dream state or deep sleep. Tantric's believe that desire is the prime motivating force of the universe. Tantric's use desire as a motivating force. Desire is believed to not belong to the intellectual self but to the vibration of the person's "Charkas" or subtle energies.

Chakras are six psychic centers in the body. These centers rest in the perineum, genitals, navel, heart, throat, and between the eyes. Each center has a complex of desires associated with it. The goal of Tantra is to experience life through all these centers at the same time. When any one of the centers is blocked, it distorts desire and causes us to focus and catalyze on that chakra center and the emotional issues associated with it. We suffer seeing the world through the illusion of unbalance.

The primary tools of Tantra are the Mantra, or repeating chant or prayer, and the Yantra   a diagram or picture of a deity. The rhythm of the Mantra and the emotional tone of the Yantra move the devotee away from self-hood into the world in touch with cellular vibration and coherence. Some Mantras are chanted 125,000 times to achieve the desired effect.

After considerable individual meditation, devotees may choose to use their sexual energy to expand and open the Chakras. Special ceremonies, using rhythm, intention, and mutual support, expand sensory experience beyond normal sexual orgasm. It is believed that Shakti, the universal feminine principal, is the source of these

85

experiences. The ecstatic meditation of sex in tantra often describes avoiding orgasm. Again, we see the use of metaphor, rhythmical mantras, and gestures to augment reality to a point of polymorphic sexual plateau instead of having orgasm as a specific goal.

In Tantra as in Voodoo, the feminine auditory/tactile response is worshiped at the heart of a culturally specific ceremony. The repeated Mantra by the group, the mutual disciplined support and the emotional tone set by the ritual, draw out a diffuse sexual response in the female devotees. The Mantra itself is the rhythmic meditation. The food and wine are eaten symbolically. Rhythm, intention, and sexual energy draw the participants into a kind of cosmic psychedelic altered state, bringing everyone together as one. The element of rhythm draws sexual sensation into the metaphysical dream of the respondent. Sexual sensation and inner psychic life become one.

The mind is trained in Tantra to become a psychic tool for experiencing complete spiritual integration with erotic sensations. Tantra is a clearinghouse of mind/body issues and constraints. The tools of Tantra are the same, rhythm, metaphor, and sexuality.

Sex and Kinesthetic Symbiosis

In the West, "Belly dancing" is mostly a secondary pastime. All the attraction to costuming, contests of belly dancers, nightclub acts, and parlor jokes have degraded belly dancing to a social spectacle in the West. The name itself belies our Western influence. Early belly dancing had the social prestige of a circus side show. It has been absorbed into middle America devoid of its sexual connotations.

Long before our Western preoccupation with the vaudeville aspects of Middle Eastern dance, Middle Eastern spiritual dancing served as a way for women to balance their bodies procreative power. With the disciplined support of musicians and the group support of other dancers, dance became a prayer to the spirits through the body.

The "zaar" is a possession-or trance dance ritual practiced solely by women throughout the eleven Middle East countries (Egypt, Sudan, Ethiopia, the Arabian and Persian Gulf states) and thought to have originated in sub-Saharan Africa. The dance is performed for the purpose of getting physical or psychological relief. In the Zaar dance; genteel sophisticated rhythms, hand clapping, finger cymbals, flute, and the supportive movement of other women protected the dancer going through a transformational experience. Belly dancing in the West frowns on and fears its sexual or transformative implications.

Sandwiched between Islam and Western prudish voyeurism based on male experience, the spiritual dancing of the Middle East has been given a PG rating. The Zaar duplicates long rhythmic meditations with repetitive dance movements and coordinated breathing either by call response song cycle or by mantra like abstract verbal song. This dance supports feminine consciousness with rhythmically induced micro-timing and perfect flow from repeated movement again coupled with long dance physical alterations of the nervous system.

Once rhythmically entrained and relaxed by these long rhythmic cycles and repetitive movements, there is a moment of revelation and transcendence that is both physical and mental:

"Out of respect for the jinn or spirits, and also to close herself off from outside influence, the dancer covers her face and head. Then as She begins to respond to the rhythm and the trance comes, she discards the veil and abandons herself to the power which has been unleashed from within."(Anon.) 1900, Egypt.

These special moments can allow the dancer to experience body, mind and sexual integration. Female seers, mystics, and priestesses used this energy to draw upon their spiritual knowledge. They "saw" into the fabric of time. Rhythmic relationship of everything became transparent to them. This effect is best explained by the concept of 'synchronism'. C.G. Jung termed the word to best expresses the effect of these subjective states and their relationship to events connected with them:

"Synchronicity takes the coincidence of events in space and time as meaning something more than chance; namely, a particular interdependence of objective events among themselves as well as with subjective (psychic) states of the observer." (Jung. 1950: In preface to The I Ching.)

Simply put, synchronicity implies interdependence. If every event is interdependent then you could be a "seer" by tapping into its rhythm. Synchronicity makes itself known through a subconscious sense of timing attributed to the musical mind. Many primitive cultures assumed that an emotional and mental intention at the moment of musical transcendence controls the very structure of the body/mind interaction.

Somehow, as in hypnosis, a new imprint on the body mind is made that carries the verbalized projection. You become one with your emotional goals and ideas. The result allows you more freedom of body movement, heightened sensory awareness, ease of activity, less stress, greater coordination, and more intuitive awareness towards your set of goals. When inner (kinesics and musically triggered hormonal response) and outer (repetitive injunctions and group support) life are in harmony, one reinforces the other. The concept of Jung's synchronism is the same as African "crossings" and the concept of 'Ashe'.

You enter the world of synchronism through rhythm, metaphor, and sensation. We use sensation as an engine to drive metaphor and personal vision deep within our being. We use rhythm to expand the sensory experience throughout the body and reset the body-mind. Jung's synchronism brought shamanistic philosophy to the psychiatrist's couch.

The study of musical sexuality has all but been ignored. We treat the musician as our Gods. We have forgotten that communal music made us whole and complete, not the musician. The sexual impulse and

89

sense of coherence is in the music, not in the musician. Consequently the Zaar arose as a completely feminine experience.

Mojo or Ashe Perfect Timing

Many dance cultures embrace myths of ideal male lovers that include musical courting and seduction. Music becomes the medium of ideal love between partners. The male lover/gods of dance culture myths teach each culture the value of subtlety and timing in integrating with the feminine. With shamanistic awareness, sexual courtship includes rhythm, musical tone, ideal timing, compassion and emotional ecstasy.

Groupie culture vies for the chance to give the secular rock elite a sexually nuanced advantage over other males. But sex without discipline and cultural context has only fleeting meaning. Myths stand as evidence to a higher male consciousness associated with music and sexuality. It is one filled with male understanding of feminine diffuse sexual impulse and psychic transcendence. Not only does the musical male lover seduce women but also in myth he seduces nature itself as with Krishna's flute.

In Voodoo, it is Legba, the master of the crossroads, the supreme Sun God that joins Erzuli the goddess of the moon and waters. Legba is the gatekeeper, the door opener into the world of mystical love and spiritual transcendence. When Legba possesses his human host, he often will act out sexually. Again, music and male sexuality are inseparable.

" *Legba is the patron of the universe, the link between the Godhead and the universe, the umbilical cord that connects the universe to its origin. Bondye fashioned the universe, Legba has nurtured it, fostered its growth, and has sustained it. His veve (prayer flag) contains the symbol of his sexual completeness, and he is invoked in matters related to sex.*"
(Leslie G. Desmangles- The faces of the Gods.)

To learn the cross rhythms is to begin to know the psychic crossroads. Rhythm is everything to Voodoo. To know rhythm is to walk with the gods. To be one with Legba is to feel the perfect moment of love almost like magic. Rhythm becomes life, rhythm becomes its own ethos. If someone has received Legba everything he does becomes seductive. Legba allies himself with the person. The person becomes rhythmically perfect. Everyone and everything is seen as in the process of falling onto place.

Like Krishna nature responds to Legba. In black lore the crow is often associated with Legba. Legba is an intermediary between nature and man. As a drummer calling Legba, you must allow him to enter your drumming to 'open the gate' to the spirit world. You must be awake in both worlds melding the rhythms of both.

Legba is often seen as a trickster hustler or charlatan. He is the "boogie" man. He is the "Smooth Criminal" in Michel Jackson's video that in slow motion throws the coin from across the room into the Juke box. With a couple tips of his hat he trances out a room full of people. The smooth criminal is Legba. He is outside our laws answering only to the rhythms of life. Legba is synchronism. Legba knows the gravity of rhythm.

Calling Legba with the rhythms isn't about showing off rhythmic prowess. It's integrating everything the drummer hears and becoming perfectly on time for those around you. Legba creates change, integration, and release. He is the sensibility of Jazz playing applied to life.

Legba's identity has been twisted so that he represents the devil. But actually Legba represents the antithesis of the Devil. The Devil embraces chaos and fear. Legba represents rhythmical harmony and temporal perfection. Legba is perfection of "cool". He is coming from inside the fabric of time and timing.

Legba is the archetypal rhythmical lover because he is concerned with seeing integration and rhythm. His sexual awareness is different; it is completely subservient to the temporal and rhythmic experience of feminine consciousness. He assumes that sexual timing is owned by the feminine and he serves that timing with his rhythmical awareness. That is his Mojo.

Mojo is the myth of perfect male timing, and second, physical male Prowse. With deep rhythmic training you take Legba in your head. You are forged into the rhythms. Mojo is force of consciousness, "cool" as it may be, it is ultimately seductive because it reflects the female psyche.

In Voodoo you become over time one with your spiritual guide. He enters your head and stays there. You don't know about him. You become his agent and seer. You see through his eyes. In a sense you become his intermediary. You walk with Ashe, you walk with Legba.

Rhythm in African dance cultures plays a large role in defining male identity. In the developed drumming cultures of West Africa random self-centered behavior was frowned upon as being spiritually ungrounded:

"Random behavior is the exact antithesis of the ritualizing orientation. In music, random improvisation and imprecision spoil the delicate texture of the rhythms, and in society random expressions spoil the delicate structure of communication...As people participate in a musical situation, they mediate conflict, and their immediate presence gives power to personal form so they may relate to it. In Africa power is not something inherent in an individual It is the full potential of what a person can do or be, and from the African perspective, someone who "has " power is someone who is capable of directing his energies with a sense of purpose." (Chernoff, African Rhythm and Sensibility 1979)

Power from rhythmical training is not the brute force of ego but a deepening of awareness and a sense of presence. Not a presence that demands attention, but one that in the subtlety of deep psychic rhythmical understanding, draws respect.

Among the Yoruba of Africa this subtlety is the essence of understanding the Yoruba "Supreme Deity". Because Olorun their supreme deity, is not personification. It is seeing into the mastery of the skies, acting with an unseen force. Olorun is nether male or female but a vital force. Olorun is the supreme quintessence of the mastery of the instantaneous now and seeing all. Many have known Olorun. The highest women, master priestesses, the diviners, the kings, the most important chiefs all have felt Olorun. And even these leaders words transcendental, susceptible to transposition into spirit invoking and predictive experiences. Because "Ashe" literally means "So be it," or "May it happen". "Ashe" lets you see Olorun in all things and makes your every gesture predicative.

From "Ashe" you see rhythmical synchronism in everything. The world becomes rhythmically transparent. To have "Ashe" is to be rhythmically enlightened. So instead of a random self-centered awareness you are coated with the effects of how rhythmical practice has changed you. You don't understand "Ashe" until you become it. From that vantage point feminine integrated sexuality becomes transparent in the moment.

For someone walking in "Ashe" completion is not seeking pleasure in the sex act but releasing bound sexual tension and subduing bio-rhythmical chaos. Thereby releasing someone that is out of rhythm with their true nature. This is the true basis of sexual healing and Legba's sexual purpose in myth.

To see through the power of "Ashe" is an attribute acquired not by intellectual observance but by practice and action. Rhythmic meditation exposes you to a personal understanding of "Ashe" and its effect on those around you.

Rhythmic kinesthesia will ground you, not in random improvisation clamoring for respect or attention, but instead in long rhythmic meditations filled with the subtlety of consciousness and physical consistency. Rhythmic grounding is not the four-minute radio groove you hear in popular music. It is the ten-hour groove of ceremony played against a poly-rhythmic and distracting background. It is a test of will. *It is the vision quest within music.*

We reach this plateau of the ancestors with practice. Your will turns the discipline of holding the groove or basic rhythm pattern from a boring exercise to a personal test of meditation and skill. Without will there is nothing gained. It is no different than the will required being a long-distance runner. The skill becomes an internal dialogue where you are exposed to the relationship between your mind's tendency to wander and your psychic presence. In seeing into time and timing itself through this discipline, you witness "Ashe" and absorb its power. You don't read about "Ashe", you soak it up like a sponge slowly through rhythmical meditation.

Playing rhythm for dancers makes you observant. Supporting the micro timing of each move with the subtlety of attention and emotional control allows you to forget your own needs and desires. The drummer's emotional empathy expresses out through the rhythms. He safely envelops the dancer encouraging them to go within. With "Ashe" desire and ability must be centered on psychic expansion, kinesis, and rhythmic support.

Inside this support the power of timing in love unfolds. Everywhere rhythmical awareness is validated by the feminine, not manifested as a rash of many lovers but as subdued mutual

95

understanding and emotional validation. The drummer meshes into womens ignored longstanding creative awareness of metaphysical feminine timing. Sex within "Ashe" is like no other sex you have ever had.

So now you can see the importance of my lengthy discussion at the beginning of this book about the nature of time. Time itself is just a ripple in the reflection of Olorun's great sea. Rhythm will show you Olorun's vastness in the universe that is now. There is no past or future. Walk with Ashe and know the present.

Live Music Vs. Sampled Music

One hundred years ago there was only live music. We have made a tradeoff. Music has become infused into our lives everywhere. But we have made a Faustian choice between music on demand and live performance. Our ancestors had to make and invent their music in the present. Music was social experience. Music and dance inspired each other. What happens when we experience live music?

With live music there is a feedback loop in the instant moment of musical creation. We share the intricacies of timing and emotion with each other. We enter a world between cause and effect. We become the improvisation in the now. Although we have vastly benefited from music on demand, we must remember that no musical performance is ever the same twice. It is always in the now. It is always connecting our communal consciousness. When we listen to a tape or CD we are listening to a remnant of a past musical experience. What is lost is our shared sense of giving to the center of the experience.

What is gained by infinite perfect repetition of recorded musical tracts? Without live emotive cultural support and the metaphorical focus of myth to guide us to musical transcendence we are as Westerners severely challenged to make any sense of our inner musical dialogue.

For men this is further a challenged, because to inspire feminine diffused eroticism through music invites exploitation. Without respect for the diffuse states themselves, there is little to prevent abandonment of respect for the subtlety of experience and to plunder it sexually. This is the antithesis of compassionate awareness of the healing act through 'Ashe' that would control the rhythmical shaman's motivations and actions.

To compassionately know the temporal magic of love is to see into all that is feminine and to be acknowledged constantly. In a look, a glance, a sigh, a movement, constant affirmation is everywhere. You start with a musical model for love; support, rhythmical consistency, sharing and improvisation. But you evolve beyond that because of the physiological changes to mind and body that music embodies.

Seeing with rhythm evolves over a period. Finding your rhythmical self creates subjective alterations in consciousness that instill emotional control or "cool". This cool is not lack of interest but awareness of subtlety. You know the saying, "He's a real player."

Playing rhythms is like meditating. You cannot play and think at the same time. You must develop the motor skills for the rhythms to become a natural part of you. Like any other motor skill this takes practice. Over time, the dynamics of the rhythms, tonal quality, tempo, and volume become part of your knowledge. Watching dance from your meditative rhythmical mind will let you start really seeing the effect your musical sense of center has on dance

Rhythms during this period are committed to kinesthetic memory. They become pure motor skill and accomplished playing is natural and relaxed. This period takes for most people several years. Motor skills require practice to achieve proficiency. Rhythm and timing is no exception.

Learning about drum shapes, styles of playing and tonal quality are natural antecedents to developed rhythmical interests. But most importantly we develop meditative rhythmical ability. The ability to hold controlled precisely articulated rhythms for a long time without falling off them because of some mental distraction or outside influence. It is this type of consistency that is needed to create the rhythmical safety that supports diffuse erotic release associated with musical sexuality.

The cross-rhythms. When multiple rhythms are played with each other, the dancer or listener is drawn into a meditative state to bring the several rhythms to unity in the mind. It is in this way that African music encourages musical meditation. The 'crossroads' in

African lore is the cross rhythms. Here is where you meet your fate.

The interweaving of diverse and multiple rhythms is coherent only when you actively participate in maintaining a point of reference in perceiving the conflicting rhythms as an ensemble. Western interpretation of rhythm is linear, African interpretation of rhythm is relational.

"An African musician accentuates and changes musical phrases, pressure on the rhythmic relationships of the ensemble, and on the dynamic qualities of transitions. By choosing rhythms which will relate clearly to the other rhythms, by controlling the duration of a rhythm, and by timing the introduction of discontinuity to his beating, he creates with a mind to generating and coordinating an expression of maximum power and vitality" (Pierce, African rhythm and Sensibility).

Out-time grooves or pulsing of on-time and out-time Polyrhythms are found in many of the rhythmical dance forms utilized to achieve trance states. The male drummer develops a meditation for playing where you must both listen and not listen at the same time. You must split your attention inside your thoughtless meditation needed to play rhythm. You become a mediator of the experience drawing unity to it through your meditative clarity of mind and willfulness.

From this split-mindfulness you pass through your own personal growth of consciousness to where there is no battle in holding your support groove while listening to and supporting the rhythms and dance movements around you that are alien to yours. You become an interloper blending disharmonies. Your understanding of your rhythmic participation becomes relational and fluid in the moment.

How does this affect your sexuality? By reading the relative and relational aspects of music, women naturally become more attracted to you. They are attracted to your meditative and relational qualities. Drumming forges you into this aspect of yourself. You have become 'cool' in the African sense. At this point after drumming for several years you start to see other aspects of the drummer's mind.

Using Hypnotic Dropouts

From the Ghost dance of the Sioux:

"She is now standing with the medicine man, who gives his whole attention to her, whirling the feather swiftly in front of her eyes, away to one side or upward into the air, waving his hands before her face as though fanning her and drawing his hand slowly from the level of her eyes away to one side or upward into the air while her gaze follows it with a fixed stare. All the time he keeps up the Hu! Hu! Hu! while the song and dance go on around them without pause. For a few minutes she continues to repeat the words of the song and keep with the step, but in a staggering drunken fashion. Then the words become unintelligible sounds, and her movements violently spasmodic, until at last she becomes rigid with her

100

*eyes shut or fixed and starring.' (**The Ghost-dance Religion and the Sioux Outbreak of 1890** by James Mooney,)*

The rhythmic shaman in this description has meditative knowledge of how to facilitate hypnosis inside rhythm. His feather-work, his handwork, and voicing break the subject's relationship to the music. It drives them deeper into a personal meditation and dream. The subject's confusion turns into emotional release. There is no intellectual methodology for this kind of knowledge. It comes through meditation, practice, and emotional centering.

The musical Shaman walks around the edge of the circle; the hypnotist like Mesmer watches his subject's concentration; the faith healer picks people out of the audience; each according to their own special training.

In their special training they have learned to create a double bind. The hypnotist skips a number; the Indian Shaman passes a feather across the visual field of the devotee; the Mambo waves a handkerchief and talks in "language" over the devotee; the faith healer grabs the top of the head of the praying person. All musical or hypnotic healers share special timing and perceive their subject's weakness or conflict. The healer rocks the boat of perception. This sensory double bind activates going within and induces at times, polymorphic sexual release.

The subject can only go two directions. They can either abandon the rhythm of which they are so much a part of or shut out the sensory disturbance that is creating the double bind. To stay inside the rhythm of the experience they must go within to avoid the

Shamans disturbance. They are "cleansed" by their own response, while being safely supported by the group music and movement. The transparency between reality and dream allows a personal dialogue with one's own sensations to split the fabric of normal experience. Waves of sensation rise through the body, engulfing the self in reverberations of diffuse pleasure and emotional clarity. These experiences heal our mind and body. Not buy outside intellectual intervention but by honoring inner dialogue. You selfheal in a moment of inner truth. There is no confessor or judge. There is just emotional and physical release and sympathetic acknowledgement

Knowledge of Entrainment.

The speed of your sensory input is variable. If you have at some point the opportunity to lay beneath a rotating ceiling fan perform the following experiment for yourself. Make sure the fan is rotating at a slow speed and observe the blades for a few minutes. Now breathe in and out very slowly and completely. While you are breathing watch the apparent fan speed. It will seem to seed and slow up with your breathing cycle. The fan speed is constant. Your perceptions are variable.

Our conscious mind "photographs" what we see at varying speeds. This variation in perceptual speed is an important in group musical settings. With the correct repetitive stimulus, the brain will synchronize it's perceptive "photographs" with the musical stimulus as the perceptual guide. In tribal music, the repetitive rhythms entrain perceptual variation. Rhythm and movement over a period synchronizes perception. This is a natural occurrence and is ordinarily called entrainment. Entrainment is the body's own high level of anticipation for the established order in perception. Entrainment takes the groups common emotional and rhythmic support into the individuals physiological awareness. Rhythm and movement bypass the higher functioning of the mind and synchronize unconsciously all the participants through kinesis or stimulation at the nervous systems stimulus-response level.

Various ethnographic accounts indicate that group sensory synchronizations at this level take from one to three hours to achieve in a live musical setting. At this point the stimulus response of our muscles and auditory filtering draw us into deep unity with each other. We are entering the common dream-echoes of shared perception.

Our perceptive "photographs" become one with the music. Our body awareness, breathing, heartbeat, conditioned movements, auditory stimulus, and sight all unify with the communal support. Our sensory landscape mimics the music. Perception rides the rhythm as our movements do. Our dreamtime now has complete support, communal and physiological. At this point group support is physical, emotional, and symbolic.

As an example, lets imagine that twenty people are lying under the same ceiling fan mentioned earlier. Everyone watching the fan is breathing together, moving together, and putting their breathing inside the rhythm of an auditory stimulus. Let's assume they do this for two hours. Eventually they will all be experiencing the motion of the fan the same. As with all-natural systems, homeostatic order is built into our biological design. This tendency toward natural order among viewers of the fan causes entrainment of sensory time.

We live constantly in the censored echo of our original perception. We are watching sort of an instant replay of the world around us, that is, until we bridge through repeated rhythm and movement into our automatic stimulus-response consciousness of 0.2 seconds. I suggest here that the repeated stimulus of sound and motor movement blend our conscious awareness with our motor responses. As a group we experience a perceptual singularity. We become instantaneously connected in the moment without lingering thoughts.

When group entrainment occurs, music and movement bypass our cognitive filters. Consciousness then bridges into the "real instant" residing in the instantaneous response of our nervous system. It is here that we are finally able to perceive in the real time of our nervous system the world around us. This is the true meaning of the word spontaneous, or in the moment. It is the essence of improvisational music.

Quite often musicians will experience a musical flourish that no one is responsible for. It just happens and surprises everybody after the fact. Jazz itself is based on these embellishments. Our mental filters that sensor our perceptions are turned off. We begin to perceive as a group, a common physiological instant caused by the rhythmical auditory response. No longer does our mind filter our connection with the external world and with each other. It is from this experience that our subjective or personal world is altered. We experience a mind-altering state of consciousness.

Music and dance take us to the edge of our shared perceptual awareness. Sex that follows the creation of perceptual singularity between musician and dancer is open, irrational, and primal. It is what our parents warned us about. Music opens an altered state of consciousness that lets us really perceive each other in the broader sense. From the musical perspective, timing and rhythm become an abstract sexual ethos. Quite often we are emotionally governed by abstraction, nuance, poetry, and music. Music opens the perceptual doors of our intuition. Shared awareness becomes a real emotional high.

Endorphin Timelines

After a considerable period of movement of over thirty minutes, the muscles of the body build up lactic acid and become fatigued. Increased circulation and metabolism counter this fatigue.

Rhythmic movement helps us overcome fatigue. The brains own protective mechanisms naturally drown out fatigue signals after a period of repetition. The brain counters muscle fatigue by sending out chemical regulators in the circulatory system that regulate the perception of pain. These regulators are called endorphins. They are specialized chemical protein messengers that account for specific neural functions.

Endorphins are neurotransmitters released in response to continuous relaxed aerobic exercise.

Endorphins sometimes cause the euphoria felt by distance runners and athletes who extend themselves for a long period of time. Continuous aerobic activity can cause endorphin release. They message our sensory wiring to be ready for pleasurable experiences and block painful ones. After a long evening of dance our perception becomes positive and pleasurable due to endorphin release.

Endorphin release enhances pleasurable sensations. Pleasurable sensations seem to be more conductive in the body. Pleasurable sensations become less localized and blend with other body perceptions more readily. Endorphin release makes you feel "blissed out" or euphoric. This euphoria is heightened by sex. Sex becomes twice the turn on. The African term we have ingrained into contemporary American culture that exemplifies endorphin release is the term "funky" or "funk". "Funk", means in translation "positive sweat".

To get funky is to put out "positive sweat" or sweat enhanced by endorphins and sexual pheromones. We send out a kind of smelly signal that we are ready to experience a real sensual high. This is not work sweat or fear sweat it is "positive sweat". When music is funky it encourages you to become "funky" yourself. Funky is not a negative term to the Afro-American musical genere. It is a positive signal that we are ready to get down. You can't get funky dancing to a three-minute single. It takes some time, like an evening of club dancing.

Funky sweat is endorphin enhancement signals within your sweat. At this point You have been group entrained, your sensory perception has been altered into a communal whole, your neurons are endorphin enriched, and like in Michael Jackson's, Smooth Criminal, someone snaps his fingers just right and trigger's your pent-up release. As depicted in the video, you drift off into a swoon.

All Dance is Ritual

The language of our movements says as much about us as our appearance does. The skill with which we move is acquired. We learn a movement by repeating it over and over till it becomes "automatic". It is the same with dance. African dance or belly dance both require you to break down movement into rhythm connected kinesic sets. These sets are often choreographed in the west, but they can also be used in improvisational style. Tribal belly dance has become very popular because of it copy/follow improvisational style.

Dancing teaches us to be fluent with our body language. It teaches us to be more balanced and on time with the world in motion around us. In Dance the body floats on the repetitive movement isolations with the rhythm as support. Dancers feel subjective sensations like being beyond self and loosing awareness of time and being without fatigue. Strength comes from coherence with the rhythms. Fatigue is not felt in riding the repetitions. A marathon of dancing supports body/mind conditioning. The body memorizes its own emotional and physical high. The mind relaxes.

Negative of closed body movements editorialize the vicious circle of mental and emotional constriction. Healing is in the groove and the move. There are basic multi-cultural dance movements that are for pelvic strengthening and fluidity. There are also dance movements for upper body release. In dance these movements become part of the body language of the dancer. Their motor skill at movement is reinforced until it is as automatic as breathing. The muscular strengthening from these movements and the motor conditioning integrates the movements into the greater body language of the dancer. This has an abstract effect on the dancer's sense of well-being. Repetitive movement breaks through unconscious blocks in the dancer's self-imaging sometimes releasing emotions associated with those blocks. The dancer releases the body memory that has been held and this release reverberates into the conscious mind. It's like remembering a dream or recalling an inspiration.

Each dance culture has its own method of integrating motor movement vocabulary. Motor movement blockages are identified differently from culture to culture: "Cleansing "(Vadoun, Macumbe, Santera, etc.), and" Casting out evil spirits" (Zarr, Garabous, Stambali). In Tantric ritual it is the chakra vibration that is "cleared". Clearing through movement, our feelings and thoughts, is a form of therapy. Such techniques have been estranged from Western Society because of fear of their primal power. Limited Western spiritual traditions don't include ritualistic or ceremonial dance. Yet these religious dance forms play a large role in the beneficial effect they have on female physiology and emotional well being.

Dance Skill Sets and Procreation

In many different parts of the world, rhythm and dance has helped women prepare for childbirth, strengthen the hips and pelvis, and improve sexual response. Hip movement dances create neurological pathways that increase pelvic blood flow and mimic motions used during lovemaking. In contemporary social media this has developed into a artform and communication called 'Tweaking'. Tweaking strengthens the hips and legs, and the pelvic floor muscles to overcome incontinence and uterine distention from childbirth. It is not surprising that more ancient forms of similar dance movement sets have gained social acceptability.

The loosely structured dances of African High-Life, Calypso from Trinidad, Samba from Brazil, Merengue from Santa Domingo, Beledi from the Middle East are just a few dances that motor condition movement of the lower torso. These dances encourage pelvic motion and freedom of movement.

All these dances have similarities. First the legs are kept very slightly bent. Hip range of motion is facilitated by lifting the heel off the ground and smoothly rotating the raised hip with shuffling steps between hip moves. Such moves repeated regularly strengthen the lower body and condition the movement into the dancers' general unconscious body language.

Before modern medicine, childbirth and motherhood was a dangerous period for women. The strong survived. Dance cultures developed an exercise for the strengthening of the pelvic floor, the regular tightening of the Pubococcygeal muscle through dance. This muscle is the most important part of the pelvic diaphragm.

Without strength in the pelvic diaphragm the multiple births of earlier women could cause urinary incontinence and uterine weakening or distension. Before modern medical intervention tribal dance was a life-or-death issue for continued birthing and postpartum health. Exercise was the only preventative. There are many cultural remnants of exercises that strengthen the pelvic diaphragm through contraction of the P.C. muscle (short for pubococcygeus muscles that not only surround the vaginal opening but also support the uterus). In Yoga, breath control and tightening of the P.C. muscle are found in many Yoga exercises.

Exercises of the pelvic floor muscles in ritual dance forms come from many sources. There are many societies where religious worship took on a larger role in personal health. Rhythm, entrainment, and sensory-motor conditioning were used extensively for preventive health.

The West African Dohemy and Yoruba religions played a major role in the reformation of religious beliefs in the African New World. By integrating Christian iconography to represent their African Gods and Goddesses, traditional worship continued. In Haitian

Vadoun, Brazilian Macumbe and Columbe, the round dance was preserved. Common to these religions is the graceful dance called the "Jenvalo".

Tweaking front to back movements came from a dance called the Jenvalo. The movements of the Jenvalo dance strengthen the pelvic floor muscles by integrating breath, movement and P.C. muscle relaxation and contraction. The dance is performed either in a standing or kneeling position. On the out-breath the pelvis is tilted inward, the upper torso is arched forward, stomach muscles are tightened, and the pelvic floor muscles are tightened. On the in breath, the pelvis is arched backward and the whole pelvic area is relaxed and opened. The Jenvalo created the sensory-motor conditioning and pelvic floor strength necessary for survival and maintenance of African women. This dance or similar dances are found throughout the Americas in the transplanted ceremonial African dance religions.

In the Middle East similar body movements in belly dance are remnants of the" birth- building" dances of West Africa. The "Camel Walk" a common front to back pelvic roll with legs bent while expanding and raising, then contracting and lowering the rib cage, is commonly seen in Middle Eastern Dancing. Pelvic lifting and rotation are common to belly dance. The moves seem like sexual display, like an expression of female sexual enticement. It is more. It is an expression of procreative power and birthing potential. It is an inherited move given to us by the ancient world for protection of the birthing cycle. Tweaking seen in this context gives someone an understanding of its natural rise in popularity.

Floor-work or floor dancing has often been viewed in Western society as erotic pandering. Its role dance goes beyond Western male voyeurism. In the privacy of ritual dance, floor-work methods strengthened women for bearing children. It was often performed only in the presence of other women. Many moves in Middle Eastern floor work simulate childbirth, strengthening the pelvic floor and toning the stomach muscles. Dance was preventative health maintenance shared by the feminine community. It was also an expression of primal connection to the earth and nature. These primal birthing simulations strengthened women emotionally, giving women power and ownership of their process of procreation.

Floor work is often accompanied by slow music. This portion of the dance is called the taxeem. The slow music simulates the breathing and muscle tension of birth contractions. Movements are done in slow motion with lots of muscle tension and release preparing the mother for the dangers and rigor of childbirth. Again, there is a stigma to this kind of dance that is unwarranted when viewed from the perspective of procreative strengthening.

Dance Movement as Therapy

Certain movements of the upper body in dance can reset the abstract emotional tone of the dancer. Through the motor conditioning of long repetitive dance isolations there is shift of perception in the dancers image of self. The dancers shift is personal, wordless,

112

and the dancer owns the effect. The emotional and conditioning shift is a self-healing process. The mind/body interaction resets relation to self.

Consider the body memory of the concave or hunched in chest. Negative emotions, poor self-esteem, fear, isolation, and a sense of feeling unprotected reinforce poor upper body posture. Modern psychology attempts to recondition our self-image through "thinking about our problems" with the guidance of a trained therapist. Through dance, the emotional reconditioning works from within the sensory- motor "sets" of body language. As the "sets" alter through re-education in dance, the emotional underpinnings of positive self-imaging are reinforced empirically through physiological memory.

Some very positive African dance forms for upper body acceptance and self esteem are: theYon Va Lou- from Nigeria, the Shango-,the Bossa Nova or Samba- from Brazil. There are many more. African dances encourage restructuring of your movement patterns. This in turn restructures your thought patterns. Basically, dancing away the blues or depression.

In Middle Eastern dance, many movements encourage chest expansion, lifting, holding back the shoulders, and isolation of movement and control of the torso. Put in a supportive rhythmic setting these movements are re-programming movements for upper body release, freedom, and emotional acceptance.

Shared in all the forms of upper body dance movement is expansion of the space that the upper body occupies and opening and exposing of the chest and breast area. Movement isolations, although difficult at first, expand personal body vocabulary to include

113

the chest in the rich language of articulate motion. To 'speak' with the upper body improves breathing and diminishes body language that invites emotional dominance.

The type of memory used to remember a dance is called motor conditioning. You condition your ability to move in a certain way by repetitive movement. The body and mind work together without any conscious effort after the movement is memorized. Motor conditioning dances that improve sacral fluidity, pelvic floor conditioning, and upper body release also prepare the body for a more pleasurable erotic response. The body remembers lower body movements without any conscious effort as you expedite your sexual high.

Conditioning also opens neural pathways for letting our sensations ride our body movement. Physical sensations like sexual pleasure expand further out into our body language, motion, and timing. The drumbeats and body isolations expand pathways for pleasurable sexual experiences.

Synchronized movements to the rhythms also become 'sexual mimicry. The dancers' body responds with conditioned ease. The dances that increase pelvic floor strength increase sexual engorgement and genital response during sex. Motor-conditioned pelvic movements from dance integrate with pleasurable sensation. It gives the dancer an automatic sexual vocabulary that increases sexual responsiveness. Upper body isolations, chest expansions, and deep breathing draw sexual energy up into the emotional center. This in turn expands your sense of erotic power and personal ownership of the sexual impluse.

114

In Tantric and Pan-African spiritual sexuality sexual energy drawn up to the emotional center is commonly venerated as a pathway to spiritual understanding, and a doorway between the physical and spiritual worlds. The metaphors for this experience are found in many cultures around the world and can be viewed as a common human experience.

Kundalini and the Snake Loa

The expanded energy wave that passes up through the body has been documented in many body positive religious cultures. This energy wave has common triggers, and it has common physical effects that are shared through many different disciplines. The sexual response moves upward from the pelvic floor engulfing the whole body.

In Tantra Yoga there are many depictions of the body having three major energy currents going from the base of the spine to the r-complex, or primitive portions of the brain. They are depicted as a straight rod of light- called the Sushumina current, and two wave like currents -crossing up through the body - the Ida and Pingala currents, male and female, yin and yang currents. The wavelike currents intersect at each chakra center and are often depicted in Tantric Art.

The ceremonial motif of West African ritual dance that is most pervasive is the motif of the center pole with two snakes inscribed around it at the center of the dance circle. One snake is feminine, and the other

115

snake is masculine. The pole itself is representative of solar energy or light. The three are called the holy triad: Legba, Ieda Wedo, and Dumbala Wedo. The visual motifs and linguistic similarities hint at a common religious source between Tantra and the African drumming cultures

When these energetic pathways are shocked open in the body by specific triggers, they cause certain common sensations. The body shakes or arches with energy, apparently losing some motor control to the energy form itself. Subjectively there are common optical and mental sensations that go along with these body energies. The sensation of energy and light passing through the body along with polymorphic sexual release is sometimes experienced.

Here are the sexual triggers we have talked about come into play: <u>Motor conditioned body movements, Rhythmic entrainment, Setting of emotional tone, and Shifting perception into shared instant sensation.</u>

All these triggers change perception. The triggers mentioned move sexual sensation out into the sensory field of the total body. The visual abstraction of the body's inner energy is also a trigger. To look at a picture of the charkas is to train yourself to experience visualizing these energies within your body. The visualizations are considered prayers in and of themselves in Tantric Yoga. Essentially you are creating a backdrop for a total body experience like the one described in literature.

In the West sexual response is viewed as a genitally centered phenomena with one peak sensory high (the clitoral response the G-spot response et cetera). If we experience sexual energy as part of an expanded field of sensory awareness then it integrates body sensations, emotions, and psychic experiences into an expanded inner dialogue. This is the integration of feminine consciousness and the expression of sexual polymorphism. The mind drops into dream, and the inner waves of subtle energy, catalyzed by sexual sensation, ripple through the physical body to its' far corners. The message that remains for us to heed from ancient body positive religions of the past is the subtle relationship between psychic and physical experience and how simple conditioning and mutual support can cause profound erotic and emotional release.

Sex as Jazz

Music is ultimately a non-ego-based form of communication. Jazz music is based on improvisation; music is followed by each player's attentiveness to one another. The players pay attention to each note on the edge of the moment. Improvisation grows out of the comfort and sense of security of the player. It's balance of his or her "talent" or "training" on their instrument and spontaneous expression. We can apply this musical model of learned ingrained talent and improvisation to our sexual experience. The movement vocabulary of your body is learned through dance.

This vocabulary is improvised on through your spontaneous reactions to pleasurable sensations during sex. When you use simple rhythmic entrainment and motor conditioned body movements before sex, you increase sexual response. Partners

117

simply rehearse movements necessary to have "good sex". Entrained sex is primarily unconscious. It takes time to learn the motor language and sensory response of your partner. Rhythmical intimacy requires rhythmic practice, emotional empathy, and heightened unconscious awareness of your partner through the perceptual doors opened by rhythmical fusion.

Using rhythm and motor conditioning as sexual foreplay will bring you together with your partner from within your somatic physical response. Once you have rhythmically "dropped in" to each other you are connected to unconscious perfect timing. Your sexual energy and timing with your partner integrate. When lovers first meet, the initial focus of attention is very strong. Rhythmic entrainment and kinesthetic conditioning further leverage this attention. You lose yourself. It's ironic that we accept the idiom of "finding a perfect partner" instead of working on the nature of "perfect sharing in the now".

Courageous, perfect sharing starts with embracing the jazz model of sex. Good sex is making it happen in the moment. Of all the methods given to you in this book the one factor that will govern your success is your ability to see beyond yourself and to meet your partner halfway. Like playing jazz.

The physical supports the metaphysical or psychic connection between the two of you. Your start "crossing" each other and find yourselves in synchronistic unconscious support. Your perfect time becomes mutual. Sex charges the sense of Ashe. Your body is the instrument, and each note is a sensation. You learn entrained and coherent sexuality by accepting your body, taking care of it, and having the discipline to train to "play your instrument". Obviously, most drugs and alcohol have no role here.

Everyone learns how to ride a bike. At first you can barely balance, only going a little way before you fall off. But after a while you can ride easily without concentrating on the act of riding. You can carry a bag of groceries and ride or do tricks like riding with no hands. What enables you to do this is your ability to teach your muscles to remember complex tasks unconsciously. Sexual sensation animates motor movement. If you have a vocabulary of motor movements that increase sexual pleasuring your response will include them automatically. Motor conditioning and sexual sensation feed on each other.

The condemnation of proactive sexual movement discourages us from developing the motor skills necessary for sexual expression and encourages us to be passive sexually. We become emotionally bound up and are unable to break through the social and familial restrictions against learning these body positive motor skills. Dance inspired motor skills encourage sexual self-esteem and personal ownership of erotic response.

Rhythm and repetition in music reinforce dance motor skills. The knowledge of a movement passes from conscious effort to unconscious effortless action. The motor skills as they are practiced, pass from foreground in the mind to background in the body.

Once the motor skill becomes "background" movement, then the mind is left open to project or "dream" while the body is performing motor actions. Conditioned motor movements blend with the sexual

119

response without being consciously "remembered". The body improvises its learned unconscious motor skills on the sexual "dream".

The fine motor movements are better learned slowly. Your body is moving from point to point. The slower you go the finer the pieces of the integrated movement. Ti-Chi, the ancient Chinese form of exercise and physical invigoration, is practiced so slowly. Also, yoga moves are slow. Take your time, find a comfortable range of motion, and breathe into your movement. Your movement becomes fluid. Your sex becomes jazz.

Sexual Plateau VS Orgasm

In popular Western culture the physical state of sexual ecstasy is seen as the spasmodic orgasm lasting a few seconds. It is seen as an event to be achieved, a goal for a small moment.

Conversely, in the sacred sexuality of Tantra, orgasm is viewed as a fixed and everlasting state you tap into. It is believed to be in continuous existence outside normal perception, time, and space. Tantrics believe that when man and woman join together, they access this fixed everlasting continually existing state of pleasure. I call this accessing "Tantric Samadhi States". Hereafter referred to as TSS. The goal in Tantra is to hold open this fixed state of ecstasy for each other, not to achieve momentary orgasm in the Western sense. This would imply that the goal is state dependent memory of hormonal and bioelectrical states associated with prolonged sex.

Tantrics access this fixed state using again, rhythm, intention, and metaphor. The tantric couple uses "mantras" (rhythmic chants), metaphoric channeling (identification with the God or Goddess), and deepened emotional tone to prepare themselves to enter this fixed state. The physical experience of sex between partners is shared so they may enter "TSS". The goal is not momentary orgasm but holding open the field of awareness to both psychic and physical sensation through shared physical disciplines during sex.

Throughout Tantric discipline there is this common theme of rhythmic union, and psychic sharing. All sensation and movement are synchronized into a rhythmic cycle. The basic rhythmic cycle is chant, breath, and body motion; breath becomes an expanded measure of that beat or cycle. Rhythmic sex is driven by sexual energy itself allowing tantrics to pass together into a continuous state of pleasure.

Holding eye contact during the rhythmic sexual cycle facilitates further psychic integration. This eye contact catalyzes the psychic energy between partners. Each partner observes a small spot in the center the brow of the other. That spot is the center of psychic awareness. This also allows them to look at the whole face of their partner without wandering the eyes. Using the channeling metaphor of the goddess "Shakti" and the male metaphor of "Shiva", each tantric lover looks beyond the person they are making love to.

By using the body time expansion, (rhythmic diminutions mentioned earlier) of expanding the shared rhythm. Partners expand their physical experience to the edge of dream. With slowing down comes heightened sensory awareness. Each sensation comes full into mind. Outwardly there appears to be no motion. Inwardly, energy waves and subtle motion communicate to dream consciousness. Tantrics expand body time together in a stabilized sexual union avoiding peak orgasm as a goal.

After a certain level of psychic contact is reached by rhythmical outward sharing of eye contact, the woman lets go and acts to float on a plateau of pleasure and dream. She floats in hypnotic fixed erotic awareness slowing into the expansion of time. Her meditation centers on the paranormal with sex as a binder or catalyst.

There is a rhythmical balance between outward sharing and the inward response, shifting from one to the other, back and forth until very little outward sharing is necessary. Sexual sensation drops into dream and subtlety so fine that breath and heartbeat are all that is needed to sustain this fixed sexual state. Conditioning your body movements, rhythmic synchronization, controlled emotional intention, and time expansion are the tools used to move partners into a Tantric sexual trance.

The male Tantric experiences this state through his empathy and awareness of perfect timing in the female psyche. He enters "TSS" through observance of her expansion into a deep dreamy experience. He is nurtured by the flow of energy in her body. The bioelectrical potential between partners continues to multiply as the female partner plateaus her sexual experience and enters deep into her inner timeless world. Male tantrics experience this state through the bioenergy of the female.

Male tantrics drink the nectar of female bliss by tasting the saliva of the female that has been modified by bioelectricity and neurochemical enhancement. Often you see in Japanese erotica men drink from below the female tongue. Same with tantra. Bioelectricity and dynamic magnetic interaction can also be tasted as a quality of this sharing but is difficult to describe.

Tantric "TSS" is a physiological state lying at the center of perfect timing between two partners. The state of perfect timing always exists in the world around us. It is the intrinsic harmony of rhythm. All is one, heartbeat, to breath, to sacral cranial pulse, to tidal rhythms, to the light and dark of each day, to the cycles of the feminine and the moon, to the changing seasons, solar life, and life- birth to death. Perfect timing goes beyond the sharing of each partner. It goes beyond personal experience. It is the enmeshing of experience into the fabric of all cosmic interrelationship.

The concept of "TSS" to Tantrics and "Ashae" in the Pan-African tradition catalyzes the musical sex experience and lets us naturally inhabit perfect time and experience perfect giving of pleasure. Rhythm and conditioning will move you into deeply emotive personal sharing. Letting go of past signatures of stress on your sexual consciousness will happen naturally. We all have an uncertain growth rate here.

123

The mind/body complex has its own agenda and governing mechanisms.

TSS Triggers

TSS like states of fixed sexual plateau continued for a long time opens state dependent memory associated with cathartic experiences: State dependent memory, learning, and behavior processes are encoded in the limbic and hypothalamic systems. These loosely related systems are the major information transducers between mind and body. All methods of mind-body healing and therapeutic hypnosis operate accessing and re-framing state dependent memory and learning systems that encode symptoms and problems.

Rhythmical sex is a learned state dependent behavior. TSS sex is measured in hours instead of minutes. Different physical states cause you to remember different memories. For the most part, non-tantrics see orgasm denial as somewhat confusing. But I would suggest mutually planning long sexual experiences is only really confusing for males.

After fixed state erotic arousal has been maintained for a while just mimicking trancelike behaviors can cause you to experience them. Women have intuited their own personal inner physical triggers for release. Popular culture is filled with sexual aphorisms like: "He made time stand still." "I forgot to breathe." "I didn't know which way was up." etc. These communicate in a primitive way, through popular culture, what makes up deeply meditative sexual release.

Slowing down is trigger number one. As movement of the body is rhythmically slowed down, awareness of energy in the body is heightened. Time seems to be put on hold, which is a common physical action during orgasm. Body time expansion allows sensation and body movement to communicate with other body rhythms like breathing, and blood flow. Body time expansion allows the held thought or feeling to be taken out of ordinary time and rippled across all your sensations. Body time expansion is a moment of silence in the din of ecstasy. Practice is simple. It is the sense of floating or timelessness... Motor conditioning body time expansion gives you complete temporal range when playing with your sensations. It is that quiet moment in the music, the calm center of a sensual hurricane. Here the door is opened into the present.

Breath lock is trigger number two. Holding your breath allows another suspension of body time like the movement slowing above. As a wave of pleasure builds the gesture of breath lock lifts the psyche onto the wave of sensation in a small suspension of body time. Breath lock is again a silence that will allow you to psychically travel within your orgasm. Breath in, lock; relax. Relaxation allows you to float longer on your breath lock. Try the following simple experiment sometime: When you're in a pool dive and swim vigorously under water as long as you can. Then after a rest, try a dive and swim very slowly till you feel the need to come up for air. You can stay under water longer if you relax and swim slowly. The deeper you relax the longer you can hold your breath.

The relaxation inside breath locking will allow your sexual energy to move rapidly around your body. Super-relaxation will induce energy waves in the body. Simply illustrated, some people can relax so far that they shiver or shake with energy automatically. They feel a sensation like a wave of shivering at the edge of their relaxation.

Inner ear adjustment is trigger number three. Rolling or gently throwing the head back or from side to side momentarily upsets the sense of balance creating a physical sense of disorientation and weightlessness. The body looses for an instant the notion of what is up and what is down. Quite often this is a spontaneous response during female orgasm. Lying down comfortably with a soft shallow pillow under you head and neck. With your eyes closed, lying on your back, gently toss your head back and forth about once every three seconds. This movement will create a sensation of being slightly disoriented. This effect can be used to heighten to open the energetic door into altered polymorphic sexual state. Your balance is sensitive to changes in direction because of small crystals of calcium carbonate called "otoliths" in the inner ear, which resist change in movement. When the head is rocked, inertial resistance of the otoliths keeps the crystals in constant motion creating a sense of imbalance. This sense of imbalance effects body awareness especially when the eyes are closed. If you practice and know this effect you can use it when you are having sex.

Third eye meditation is the fourth trigger. Close your eyes. As you look slightly up between your eyes you will feel a peculiar sensation in your mind space. Your mind

126

space will seem to occupy more imaginary volume. Look here in a relaxed manner. Mixed with erotic pleasure looking here will be a trigger. Orient yourself with the "Ajna" exercise while you are in a normal physical state so you can reconnect with it when you are in a fixed state of sexual arousal. During arousal as a wave of pleasure engulfs you shift the energy into the "Ajna" meditation and then back to eye contact with your partner in cycles synchronized with your sexual release.

Super relaxation is the fifth trigger. Super relaxation is a conscious effort to relax all your musculature at once like the yoga meditation of successively relaxing each part of your body. With long periods of sex, there is a constant state of sexual neuromodulation and bioelectrical capacitance. Deep relaxation in this altered consciousness triggers physical symptoms that are embodied with myth and symbolism.

Shaking, arching, waving, or vibrating sensations can be felt as the energy waves in the body. They come and go, coursing through the body. They are caused by chemical modulation of the nervous system due to extended sex. Movements expressing inner energy can also be motor conditioned in a normal waking state to be later mimicked on the edge of sexual transcendence. A mimicked response can spontaneously shift into an uncontrolled ecstatic convulsion when it is washed over by the sexual energy in the body. Arching and involuntary muscle contraction is seen in many rhythmic ceremonies where trance induction is occurring as in Voodoo. It is also quite often part of the feminine orgasmic response and considered normal.

In Western society, arching is often depicted in erotic photographs or suggestive advertising. Photographs of the arched female in a seductive pose is a subliminal cultural lesson in the experience of subtle experience of energetic sexuality. Shaking is often heard of in the description of trance experiences. The religious movement called the Shakers received their name because of the shaking trances that their congregations would fall into. Shaking too is a common physical response for many women during orgasm. A woman will often uncontrollably shake at the peak of her orgasmic experience.

Waves of release may pass through the body like an induced ripple in a bolt of silk. The sensation may include feeling the energy escape right out the top of the head. When experiencing a sexual body wave, previous dance conditioning from movements isolating the upper and lower torso will ease the physical expression of the subtle energy passing up through the body. You can learn to articulate your body's ecstatic energy release and map your bodies' response to it.

Affirmations Inside Sexual Plateau

Sex is by its physical effect a transformation of the body-mind matrix into an altered state. During this altered physical state, you are communicating with ancient portions of the mind and their relationship with the bodies functioning. You are communicating with

128

your internal rhythms and the rhythms in the world around you. It is important that your guided meditation be loving and positive. It is your connection to the creative process from within the crossing point of your sexualized neurological state. From an emotional context, it is the magical moment in body positive spiritual awakening.

Your thoughts are little psychic guides into your perceived rhythmical sexual perfection. If you hold a mental image it will seem to expand out across time and space. Sex mingles with affirmation. Your state exists as cohabitated instant synchronicity in the instant with your partner. Prepared affirmations can be used to imprint on the mind/body complex.

So, if you pick a thought like visions of nature, abstract visualizations of healing, visualization of personal unity, chakra energy, or whatever you are aspiring for, your partner with gentle dialogue can affirm you. The images can be a scene, projected sexual experience, or expanded fantasy with your partner. It is like dirty talk but more sophisticated and more effective for personal transformation. Your conscious mind projected into rhythmical sexual response communicates with the ancient unconscious layers of the primitive mind. Holding of a mental image or thought during orgiastic response transcribes it into the body/mind complex of what we call consciousness. Thought and orgasm reset and crystallize personal will, a positive reward for a positive thought. It is classic behavioral conditioning using extreme pleasure as the associative relation to the idea or motivation desired. Later, when in an ordinary state of consciousness, the suggested motivation is associated with sexual plateau and is unconsciously activated. We are all familiar with sexual verbalization for heightened sexual pleasure. Verbalization is used to communicate to a partner, to direct bold physical attention and sensation towards a common orgasmic goal. The passionate female partner uses it to excite and direct.

Erotic communication between partners of a shared fantasy excites the psychic and sensual momentum of the couple. The shared momentum feels like an empowerment that drives physical sensation forward. Greater, expanded sexual power comes from the quality of it being shared, or recognized by someone else. These communal expressions are used for ends beyond sexual satisfaction in body positive cultures. Mental projection and verbalization is used together in Tantric sexuality in the common chanted mantra and mental projection towards the worship of one of the Tantric God or Goddesses.

In Macumbe, Santera, and Voodoo there are rituals that use polymorphous orgasmic projection to captivate and talk to the Gods or Goddesses. When the participant is possessed by a Loa, Orisha, or Bori, they communicate through them, and through their human intermediary's orgasmic state. In these orgasmic rites, physical effects of voice vibrations on the upper body resonate with the ambient communal sounds: chanting, ritual rhythms, and communal song or clapping. Surrounding sounds and vocalizations phase locking with the orgasmic participant's vocal vibration in the chest cavity induces the progression of sexual energy throughout the body. This amplifies sound making the vocalization more resonant in the body. The added resonance refocuses sexual sensation in the chest and throat often triggering strong emotional reactions associated with the mental image or metaphor. In the instant of release, diffuse feminine sexual energy unleashes directed psychic energy to the core of personal perception. The symbolism is a ceremonial activation point that gives this sexuality both boundaries and group context.

Your own private fantasy is the most personal form of orgasmic projection. You use fantasy a fantasy to enhance a sexual experience. You use mental fantasy to enhance orgasmic triggers. The personal goal of a heightened sexual experience is satisfied. Directed fantasy alters sexual perception and proclivity. But fantasy and sexual orgasm integrated together can be expressed beyond someone's personal sexual goals as an outward social gesture. It can extend to the projection of a task to be accomplished, a healing act, encourage enrichment or growth, be in sympathy with seasonal rhythms, honor a particular deity, or to create an expanded connection to your lover.

Orgasmic projection can expand personal goals into integrating the cycles of nature. The May pole dancing and nocturnal liaisons of the first day of spring attest to our primitive sexual nature conjuring of old. It has been the focus of many feministic nature religions. Orgasmic conjuring was used to attest to nature and the originating rhythm of creation. In an abstraction of creative joy, there is a marriage of natural environmental cycles and individual biorhythms of women. This was the Goddesses relationship with nature. It was a sexual one. Orgasmic projection has been used for spirit worship, spell casting, fetish creation, and exhibition. It survives today in the Pan

African, Celtic, and Mediterranean dance religions often cloaked in secrecy. Women have always projected their desires through their filter of pleasure. For now, orgasmic projection is hidden in the bedroom.

In the modern private use of these techniques, you inhabit rhythmical synchronism with your thoughts. You not only activate your own person but your extended relationship inside the world. Assume you say out loud "I love strawberries" during orgasm. Not only will you unconsciously desire strawberries, but the sympathetic matrix of synchronism could by odd circumstance have you a week later at a Strawberry Festival sampling hundreds of different varieties because a friend randomly gave you tickets. Again, I refer to the translated meaning of 'Ashe'. It has a double meaning of "So be it". AND "It may happen". If you strive to put yourself in the coherence of all things, then all things will possibly be in coherence with you.

Hypnotic Dropouts in the Rhythm of Touch

In hypnotic induction, when the hypnotist is inducing the subject by counting, they will "drop out" numbers in the count to trick the subject into thinking they have slept or lost themselves in the count.

In the rhythmic support of your touch, dropping out a beat at the edge of release leaves the mind of your lover to fill in the spaces. Her desire and physical experience jump out to fill the vacuum of that one missed beat. The absence of that one missed beat can cause expressive sexual release.

Before the dropout became the tool of modern psychology and hypnotism, it was the tool of the Shaman. Like the body time expansion and the breath lock, dropout is a suspension of time where silence is displaced by your partner's inner experience of cosmic time. In this tiny silence of your touch, she can "hear" the energy within herself filtered through her desire and dream. Finding that special moment for her rests with you and your compassion to see. The drop out creates a sensual vacuum that is met and filled with desire.

Rhythm in its' complexity beyond written timing can push and pull against the background beat, falling a bit after or a bit before the percussive instant. The body in motion expresses the rhythmic cycle. Touch confirms perfect time and motion. Quite often in books on Tantra there are references to being in a sexual state together without movement. Partners often float motionlessly within a larger sexual cycle that includes active stimulation.

Afterglow

Sometimes the shift of emotionally deep polymorphic sexual response occurs in the quiet moments after a long plateau of fixed state pleasuring during a period of quiet bonding. Sometimes dream response occurs on the brink of sleep. Here forsaking male orgasm allows men to be in a more emotionally sympathetic state with the feminine.

In the quiet moments when erotic plateau gives way to dream and relaxation, touch plays a remarkable role in bonding and emotional release. Touch becomes the conformation of inner experience in its subtlety. Taking time to silently bond with your partner gives shared body-rhythms a chance to integrate between partners in bioelectric nuance. It is part of the totality of the rhythmical partnership. Quiet bonding synthesizes mood and feeling between partners as the body-mind integrates and absorbs. The quiet moments are for absorption and weaving of physical states between partners by micro vibration. Often our lives are too complex and timed out to experience these languid states together. Take the time. Always be the best lover you can be.

After the longer sensual plateau, the body releases positive pleasure-oriented neurotransmitters into the circulatory system. Beta-endorphins and natural opiates cluster throughout the body and cross-reference to all the bodies major functioning systems during this stupor phase of sex. Neurotransmitters should be given time to reset the body's biological clocks. Rest will open the body to experiencing the delicate moods induced by neurotransmitter release. Rest or sleep together will entrain your biorhythms with your partners. Sex bonds your bodies with cosmic or natural time. Sounds too out there. But let me explain.

The hypothalamus, limbic and pituitary portions of our brains are the oldest. These portions of the brain are deep in the center of our larger more recent brain. They are the control center that orchestrates our body's rhythmical biological activity. From these ancient control centers over 200 different types of neurotransmitters are sent through the body's fluids to specific 'addressed' sites where they cluster. In much the same way a letter is mailed to a fixed location, neurotransmitters are labeled for specific locations in the nervous system. Once they get to their destination, they control the traffic of nerve impulses altering perception and controlling biological activity.

All the automatic activity of the body is orchestrated in an intricate interlacing of biorhythms controlled by the timely release of neurotransmitters in this chemical signaling process. Our health and wholeness depend on this rhythmical orchestration. Breathing, heart rate, digestion, sleep, emotional balance, sexuality and health are all controlled by this message system. When the body/mind perceives peace and outward consistency in the rhythmic fabric of life it reinforces these inner timekeepers and entrains them to the outside world.

Stress and Beyond

When the body reacts to a stressful situation, it thinks it is reacting to a one-time event. Many of the bodies' ongoing biorhythms are shut down to deal with the singular stress event. The most predominant neurotransmitter during a stressful event is one called epinephrine (adrenaline). It is addressed and sent to be released into the bloodstream to increase metabolism, shut down the digestive system, depress the immune system, and cause a state of mental agitation or anxiety to protect ones self from the stress coming at them.

If outside stress events become regular, we degrade our body-minds ability to synchronize our body-rhythms. The body becomes conditioned to the stress response. We habituate the stress response. Continual de-integration of our body rhythms by habituated stress response slowly makes us ill.

S tress and Digestive Rhythms: When our digestive rhythms are deregulated by continued stress we can experience eating and elimination disorders; diarrhea, constipation, stomach ulcers, self-starvation, binge eating and bulimia are the most common. When we experience a stress state, our digestive system is shut down to allow our physical resources to be used on increased metabolism and heightened awareness of our external environment. Continued stress deregulates our digestive cycles causing lack of appetite or acidulation of the stomach.

S tress and sleep rhythms: We also have rest and awake cycles that are deregulated by constant stress. "Ultradian" (90 to 120 min. cycles of restfulness and activity) and Circadian (24-hour cycle of sleep and wakefulness) cycles that are interfered with cause: fatigue, mood swings, and lack of sleep, listlessness, apathy, suggestibility, and nightmares. Interfering with sleep rhythms has been used as a form of brainwashing. Constant stress that interferes with sleep can have the same effects.

S tress and Sexual Rhythms: Stress acts on sexual rhythms and reproduction by interfering with rhythmical hormonal release. In women the chemical messengers for a balanced female cycle are thrown off

136

creating hormonal and fertility imbalances with common symptoms: irregular periods, cramping, false pregnancy, P.M.S., headaches, infertility, early menopause, and lack of orgasmic response.

In males excessive stress response can cause decreased sex drive because of unbalanced hormonal production. Constant stress can decrease male sex drive and cause temporary impotence. For both sexes this is a successful adaptation to a stressful environment, causing fewer births and lowered population rates during a long-term contact with a negative environment. For the individual it clouds positive sexual experience by slowly diminishing sex drive.

S tress and the immune system: Constant stress decreases immunity. Specialized cells of the immune system like T-cells, B-Cells, Monocytes, Neutrophils, and Killer cells create, release and absorb neurotransmitters that mediate communication with the endocrine (glands) and central nervous system. Constant stress reduces "all is well" neurotransmitters (like endorphins and natural endo-opiates) in the blood stream signaling the immune system to reduce the healing process to accommodate the bodes stress state.

Stress and Circulatory Rhythms: Stress increases heart rate and raises blood pressure. Commonly people with allot of stress have high blood pressure. Meditation and breathing techniques have been shown to reduce blood pressure. Women generally have less stress related circulatory problems. Their bodies are not predisposed to live with continued stress states. The hormonal balance of the monthly fertility rhythm and birthing cycle overrides these states. Estrogen, a female sex hormone, whose production is triggered by gender based genetic encoding has been shown to reduce circulatory problems and heart attacks.

Stress and Breathing Rhythms: Stress response interferes with breathing depth and regularity. Rapid shallow breathing is associated with stress or shock. Breathing inefficiency during a stress event lowers oxygen content in the blood and can cause someone to "pass out" due to lack of oxygen to the brain. Stress can also cause someone to hyperventilation or over breathe. The natural relaxed even breath is broken by stress.

Rhythmical and sensual polymorphic healing accesses cognitive awareness and networked consciousness from several different directions at once. Rhythmical meditation, rhythmical motor conditioned movements, and directed visualization shift ancient brain center neuro-addressing into a positive pleasure oriented integrative state. Synchronization of consciousness into rhythmic patterns causes brain waves to change. Beta waves, brain wave patterns usually associated with stress shift toward the alpha, delta, and theta brain wave patterns usually associated with sleep, relaxation, and sexual response.

Repetitive movement creates neural paths in the higher brain centers that stimulate the hypothalamic-limbic-pituitary complex. The complex initiates the pleasure response by releasing addressed natural opiates into the body fluids that are "mailed" to selective sights throughout the body. Upon receiving these opiates, body functions are shifted to a new expression of networked consciousness based on coherent sensing and the opened pleasure response.

"All the homeostatic internal regulatory centers from the spine up through the brain stem, pons, thalamus, and hypothalamus are in communication with this vast sexual receptor system. All major behavioral states of attention, motivation, sleep, dream, memory and learning are likewise involved." (Mind-Body Therapy by Rossi & Cheek, 1988)

Made in the USA
Monee, IL
12 October 2024

67769734R00079